VINCENZO VENEZIA

dismissive avoidant attachment

Stop Ignoring your Emotions, Shorten Distance in Relationships, and Cultivate Emotional Intimacy without Feeling Trapped

TABLE OF CONTENTS

INTRODUCTION

Love is a wild, unpredictable mystery. You never know what it will bring or when it might strike. Sometimes, you can fall in love instantly when someone smiles at you. Other times, you may search for years before finding someone who makes you happy. There are moments when life is simple and moments when it is difficult. But one thing is certain: love can change your life forever.

People have a wide range of ideas about what love should be like and how individuals should act in interpersonal relationships. Some people believe that they need to be married by a certain age. Other people believe they shouldn't be in a long-term relationship until they've reached a certain age, or their parents approve of it. Such beliefs and expectations rarely make for a healthy relationship.

In reality, love is an irrational and unpredictable force. One second you can be completely head over heels for someone, and the next second they could be your worst enemy. Love is unpredictable, and it's up to you to ensure that your relationships are healthy. So, what can you do? How can you make sure that your relationship lasts? Knowing yourself is the best way to know if a relationship will last or if the two of you are headed for trouble.

Our childhood experiences influence and shape us into the adults that we are. Our parents, siblings, and other relatives greatly impact how we see the world and interact with the people around us. Some psychologists believe that our attachment styles are influenced from birth. Secure attachments in childhood have been found to correlate with people who can be self-confident and assertive without being aggressive or insecure. Children with secure attachments know they can trust themselves and their people. They generally have a good sense of self-esteem, which is necessary for a healthy adult relationship.

But there are other styles of attachment – other ways our brains interpret things around us. These ways of thinking can manifest themselves in our relationships with others, how we love, and how we feel about ourselves.

Dismissive avoidant attachment is a particular attachment style that many people have. Dismissive-avoidants tend to be self-centered and highly anxious. They also tend to be distrustful of others. They put up walls in a relationship to protect themselves and their feelings. This kind of behavior prevents them from ever truly opening up to their partners for fear that they might get hurt. It also prevents them from developing a deep trust with the other person.

The way they love will be different from someone with secure attachment. This book will help you to understand the many things that someone with dismissive avoidant attachment might do in a relationship, why they do them, and what you can do about it if you're in love with a dismissive avoidant.

You'll learn about the types of things that are likely to go wrong in your relationship, and you'll learn how to make your relationship more secure. You can incorporate some of these tips into your love life even if you aren't already in a relationship.

PART 1

AN INTRODUCTION TO DISMISSIVE AVOIDANT ATTACHMENT

CHAPTER 1

WHAT IS ATTACHMENT THEORY?

The formation of emotional bonds is the subject of attachment theory. People learn to build and maintain relationships primarily through early interactions with a parent or other primary caregiver, who becomes the prototype for all later adult relationships. Attachment theory is based on observations of infants and animals that have been raised in groups where there is a clear hierarchy.

Attachment results from evolutionary processes that began thousands of years before humans developed the ability to talk or think. As long as our prehistoric ancestors lived in their natural environment, they could survive with only rudimentary skills such as hunting and gathering food. But the advent of agriculture changed the nature of society. Cultivating crops required labor and produced a surplus that could be stored for times when there was no food or shelter. And as social groups became larger during the Neolithic period (the period between 10,000 and 5,000 BC), they needed to develop more complex systems for integrating their new, expanded resources.

When early humans first began herding and breeding domestic animals, they had to establish a new system for managing relationships between people and their animals. As long as the humans were dispersed in small nomadic groups, the animal herd was unnecessary because the meat was easily obtained by hunting alone. But once herders started tending more than one animal, they needed a more complex system of social organization. The birth of agriculture caused a rapid increase in population numbers and increased conflict among groups that contested grazing rights. Communication could not resolve these issues – so conflict became endemic to societies that developed agriculture and organized political systems.

The overwhelming conclusion was that a system of communication was necessary to help manage the relationships between humans. Communication is key to managing relationships, whether by gestures or small tools. This paves the way for our present-day societies in which massive numbers of communities have evolved through the social and political organization. It is also the foundation of all human development – including emotional development.

As part of the human race, we are taught to have a sense of being an individual, independent from others – but this is quite an illusion because we are highly interdependent creatures. According to attachment theory, this interdependence is the foundation for our relationships with others – for the success of our relationships and the quality thereof. This interdependence is what attachment theory is all about.

We develop relationships based on these emotional bonds through our interactions with others. This is how we engage with the world and other people, and the quality of our relationships is contingent upon how successfully we manage this relationship process. Through our interactions with other people, whether family members, friends, caregivers, or lovers, we develop a web of relationships that can be either positive or negative – acting as a buffer to help us manage the stressors that are placed upon us every day.

John Bowlby's Attachment Theory

John Bowlby was a British psychiatrist whose seminal work, "Attachment and Loss: A Theory of Attachment" (1969), laid the foundation of modern attachment theory. Bowlby thought that a child's early relationships with their caregivers have a profound effect that endures throughout life. He claimed that the infant's chances of survival are increased when they have a secure attachment because attachment keeps the child close to its caregiver and allows it to learn important survival skills such as coping with the environment and regulating its own emotions and stress responses. If the child does not have a secure attachment with its caregivers, it has a greater chance of developing physical, mental, and emotional problems that could last into adulthood.

The Main Points of Bowlby's Theory

There are 3 main points in John Bowlby's theory of attachment.

1. We Are Biologically Based and Wired in Our Genes

Bowlby believed that our attachment style is hardwired into our genes – and that it is not learned. We are born with certain genetic makeup. He thought this should be further researched so we may understand how attachment styles begin – and how they develop as we age. He suggested that these attachment styles are sensitive to context but not innately fixed.

To explain...

Our attachment style begins with an early bond with our caregivers. According to Bowlby, infants are biologically programmed to seek closeness from their primary caregivers in the first months of life. If this is not provided or the caregiver fails to respond appropriately to the infant's needs, the child may become distressed and emotionally disturbed. Infants might develop a series of problems, including social (such as anxiety), mental (such as depression), and physical problems later in life.

As an adult...

John Bowlby believed that attachment styles are sensitive to context. He believed that our attachment style develops slowly over time based on our experiences with our parents, siblings, friends, and caregivers throughout early childhood and adolescence. This notion is called "internal working models" (IWMs), which are defined as an individual's subjective representation of others and their range of available responses that form a subjective template of the world. IWMs result from our early interactions with caregivers, friends, and partners throughout life.

2. Infants Have an Early Need to Form Attachments or Bonds with Their Caregivers.

We are born with certain physical, psychological, and social needs which we look to our caregivers to fulfil. These needs help us manage the stressors we encounter in our everyday world. According to Bowlby, infants need close contact with a caregiver for survival and protection in the face of shock, pain, and trauma. Infants are biologically programmed to form attachment relationships that promote a sense of security – or baseline of comfort – from their caregivers and family members. If infants are not given this sense of security, they might become physically or emotionally distressed.

As an adult...

The need to be attached to others continues through life. Even though we grow and mature and have more experiences, we still need attachment with others – which is why we develop close relationships with our family members, friends, partners, and children. When this early relationship fails or is not formed, it causes disruptions throughout life.

According to Bowlby, attachment theory is a way of understanding our relationships and how we are connected. According to his developmental theory, our earliest relationships with our caregivers shape an internal working model of ourselves, others, and the world in general. For example, if our early relationship was disrupted because there was physical or emotional abuse in our household or if one or both of our parents were absent for a long period when we were young, then we could develop a negative IWM (e.g., "No one can be trusted" or "The world is not safe").

3. Our Attachment Needs Are Not Only Aimed at Our Caregivers But Also at Those Around Us.

We are not only biologically programmed to form attachments with our caregivers but also to attach to people in other relationships. As adults, we can still be emotionally and physically close to our parents, even though they no longer play such a major role in our lives. In other words, we still need to bond and attach to others just as much as we do with our caregivers. To Bowlby, this process is called emotional availability – or the state in which someone is open or ready for positive, emotional interactions with others.

Attachment theory goes beyond the traditional approaches of psychology, which analyze and study individuals' behaviors in isolation or as a part of a larger family system. It emphasizes the importance of the environment, context, and how infants interact with their caregivers – either directly by forming attachments, or indirectly when they fail to do so.

Attachment theory is a comprehensive approach to understanding how we develop relationships throughout life based on our early experiences with our caregivers. Some people have a secure attachment style, while others might have an anxious or ambivalent attachment style – which reflects Bowlby's notion that our personalities are based on how we are attach to others throughout life.

Secure Attachment in Childhood

This attachment style is based on the belief that we are safe and secure around others, including our caregivers. When we are in a secure attachment relationship with our primary caregivers, we feel that they can be trusted and relied upon. This security leads to developing a 'baseline of comfort,' which allows us to feel comfortable and confident. We learn how we feel if others are available or not available throughout life through our close relationships with family members, friends, and partners during childhood.

How Does Secure Attachment Develop?

Two conditions must be met for the formation of secure attachment:

1. Intimacy and sensitivity

Mothers sensitive to their children's needs are known as "expressive" mothers, while those not so attuned to their child's needs are known as "insensitive" mothers. While intimacy can be defined as feelings of closeness, warmth, and caring between two people, sensitivity is the ability to respond appropriately to infants' cues and signals. Sensitive mothers tend to be concerned about their infant's attachment needs and will try to understand how they might feel in certain situations, and respond appropriately by varying their behavior during interactions. Sensitive mothers will vary how they talk or play with their infant (e.g., singing to their infant if they are upset or playing peek-a-boo if they are interested or happy). According to attachment theory, sensitive mothers will likely have infants who develop a secure attachment style.

Insensitive mothers tend to be more directive in their interactions with their infants. For example, they might respond to an infant's needs quickly (e.g., feeding her), or they might not be able to notice an infant's cues at all (e.g., when an infant is crying) – which can lead to infants not feeling safe in their mother's presence. According to Bowlby, sensitive mothers are involved in their infant's social and emotional development through their interactions with them, while insensitive mothers simply feed and change their infants.

2. The Infant must feel safe with their caregiver

For an infant to feel safe with its caregiver, the infant must recognize that it is safe when the attachment figure is nearby – even if the caregiver does not make eye contact or verbally respond. Children who have developed a secure attachment style have had a sensitive and responsive caregiver attend to their needs, which allowed them to understand that others would be there for them whenever they needed them. After gaining this sense of security, infants will explore their environment with curiosity and confidence, knowing they can rely on their parents when needed.

To help their child feel secure, a parent can be sensitive and responsive to the baby's cues and give their child positive feedback when interacting with them.

The Critical Period for Brain Development and Early Childhood Education

Bowlby suggests that there is a critical period for developing an attachment. The term "critical period" in etiology refers to a specific period of an organism's early development when it learns the skills necessary for survival. These factors affect how processes like hearing and vision, social bonding, and language learning develop. A person may find it challenging or perhaps impossible to develop certain functions connected to an ability later in life if it is not exposed to the stimuli required to learn the skill during a crucial stage of its development.

The following are the critical period stages:

a. 0 - 6 Months

The first critical period for social attachment is between 0 and 6 months. During this time, the child learns to distinguish between familiar, friendly human faces and strange human faces. The child will begin learning to manage their own emotions when separated from the primary attachment figure through a process called self-soothing. The child can also learn to recognize familiar faces and voices and "coo" and "cry" in response to these stimuli.

This period allows the infant to identify emotions and signs of distress at an early stage of development, which will help to build a secure attachment base for future relationships. Suppose not enough attention or care is given during this period. In that case, the infant may not be able to develop the necessary skills or comfort level in future interactions.

b. 6 Months - 1 year

At 6 months, the child can display a very primitive form of attachment behavior. This includes looking for the face of the primary caregiver when frightened and when presented with a stranger. The child will begin acting out its own needs by reaching toward the familiar caregiver or family pet by 7 months and will show distress in response to being separated from the primary attachment figure. By 9 months, the child can identify familiar faces and voices and differentiate between strangers and those they know. Facial expression recognition continues to develop at this point as the child begins to associate faces with emotions and can learn the relationship between the two.

This period allows the infant to identify primary attachment figures and begin learning about family members through association. The infant will be able to recognize the primary caregiver and interact with them more comfortably than unfamiliar people.

c. 1 year - 3 years

By one year, the child has developed the ability to move toward certain people when they are harmed or in pain. This allows them to have a closer relationship with their primary attachment figure. The child can also differentiate between familiar and unfamiliar voices. During this period, the child is usually able to be separated from the primary caregiver for short periods without the child experiencing significant separation anxiety. If this does not occur during this stage, there is an increased chance of problems occurring in future relationships because of increased anxiety surrounding separations or social interactions.

d. 3 years - 6 years

By 3 years of age, children can maintain eye contact longer and play in groups. By this time, they will have developed a basic understanding of cause and effect. Around this time, children begin to show more independence in play and start developing relationships with other children. They start to grasp relationships more intricately and get better at inventing story characters, listening to stories and connecting them to their own experiences (a.k.a., "fictitious play"). The child can now tell different stories about familiar people and places they have experienced.

This period allows for continued growth in social understanding, which will help the child develop into a person who can interact with others in socially acceptable ways.

e. 6 years - 12 years

The final critical period of social development occurs between 6 and 12 years of age. By this time, children can understand that other people have different values, thoughts, and beliefs to them, and can create complex moral and ethical systems of rules for interaction with others. Children begin to be called "adolescents" at this age and can create their own rules for their group, which is their primary attachment base.

This period allows children to become more independent, even though the child does not yet have a fully functioning sense of self. The child may feel disconnected from others and attempt to compensate for their lack of identity by building relationships with their attachment figure. If not enough attention is given during this time, the child could be exposed to situations in which it may not be able to develop the necessary skills or comfort level in future interactions.

The Importance of Attachment Security in Childhood

The following are the reasons why solid attachments in childhood are crucial for adult relationships:

1. Good Self-esteem

Self-esteem is the sense of worth we give ourselves. Having good self-esteem is crucial because it will contribute to our future. If we do not have good self-esteem, we will be unable to accomplish goals and succeed.

Those with secure attachments will have a greater and more positive sense of self-esteem. They will feel loved by their parents, who will show them respect and care for what they do. This is because children with secure attachments grow up feeling important and good about themselves as a result of the way their parents treat them. When children feel respected and valued by their parents, they will feel more confident and can function independently at an early age. These children will usually stay away from drugs and alcohol and will likely avoid trouble. They will also be more likely to form healthy relationships with those around them, including their parents.

Securely attached children are less likely to have issues with self-esteem because they can appreciate their positives and deal with their negatives. If a child feels insecure or unloved, or if their parents do not recognize the good things they do, then the child will feel unworthy of praise. Parents need to tell their children what they are good at and give them compliments when they do good deeds. This is because children need to know that the people around them care about what they are doing. Humility is also important, as children who say that they are better than others are less likely to listen to what others say about them or their actions. In the future, these children may have issues with how they view their strengths and weaknesses and therefore will not be able to succeed in anything they do.

2. Good Relationships with Others

Children with secure attachments are more likely to have good relationships with others because they know how to form healthy bonds with those around them. They have positive views of others and form healthy relationships because they feel comfortable around others.

A secure attachment bond allows children to open up and say what is on their minds. This is because when a child feels comfortable enough to talk, it is a sign that they trust the other person. These children will not be turned off by talking to others and will respect the opinions of others. This is an important part of developing healthy relationships. These children are also less likely to do things that will hurt them or break the rules because they do not want their parents to be disappointed in them. However, if a child has an insecure attachment and does not feel comfortable talking to others, then they are less likely to have friends.

3. Good Relationships

Children who have high self-esteem get along with others well, and as adults, they are more likely to have happy love relationships. They will also be more likely to have successful careers because they will understand how important trusting and respecting others is in the workplace, their careers, and their personal life.

Those who do not trust others or do not respect their opinions are less likely to succeed in their careers because they did not learn the importance of building healthy relationships. Children need to be able to trust their parents so that they can communicate what is on their minds. This way, children who have good relationships with their parents will be able to continue having healthy relationships with others after they are grown up. Because they are self-assured and able to express their feelings to others about what they want to achieve, they will also be able to select a profession or vocation that is ideal for them.

4. Co-operation

Children with stable bonds are better prepared to deal with challenges when they arise. These children are less likely to assume that others want the worst for them and that they will be punished for doing something wrong.

Secure attachments help people deal with negative emotions and problems in the workplace and in relationships because they are less likely to assume that people who have authority over them have bad intentions. Because they do not feel uncomfortable or unimportant, they will be more inclined to cooperate with those who are in positions of authority. This is important because if people are cooperative and willing to work with those around them, their employers are more likely to give them a raise or offer benefits.

5. Enjoyment of life

Those with good self-esteem enjoy life more and are more willing to take chances because they feel confident in their abilities. They also typically have stronger connections with other people. These children love themselves for who they are, not for what everyone else thinks about them, and this is the most important part of enjoying life.

Children must have a healthy relationship with those around them, so they do not worry about saying or doing something wrong. They need to be open-minded and willing to learn new things if they want to enjoy life. If children are unwilling to listen to those around them, they will not be able to learn anything new and may resent those around them.

Due to their lack of concern about what other people think of them, securely attached children will be more inclined to explore new things and take risks. Additionally, rather than stressing about what other people think of them, they can use setbacks as opportunities to master new skills. They are aware that everyone makes errors and know that they are perfectly capable of learning from them and moving on with their life.

6. Low Stress Levels

It is more likely that children with secure attachments will have lower stress levels in the workplace and in their personal life. This is important because those with lower stress levels are less likely to get sick.

People who do not trust others or respect their opinions are more likely to experience high amounts of anxiety in their relationships because they feel insecure and do not know if others have good or bad intentions toward them. In addition to that, they are more likely to be nervous or scared during meetings or presentations simply because they do not feel confident in what they have to say. They constantly worry about what others think of them and how they can improve their work.

People who have low stress levels are more likely to have successful careers and romantic relationships simply because they are less tired and worried. They are also more likely to enjoy the things they do during their free time because they know they can get up and do something else if the work becomes too stressful.

7. Accepting People As They Are

Children that have strong attachments can accept people more readily. They are generally more open-minded and accepting of others. They will not be threatened by someone else's personality, physical appearance, or other traits that make them different from them. Children with secure attachments generally show a lot more respect for others because they know those around them want the best for them.

When children befriend others who are different, they learn to accept those differences. They also understand that the other person may have become the way they are because of their environment. These children realize that people can change if they want to, but it is up to them whether or not they wish to do so.

In the future, these children will be less likely to put others down for their differences and more willing to accept others. As a result of this acceptance, they will form more beneficial relationships with others.

8. Self-Regulation

Those with high self-esteem are better able to regulate their emotions and experiences. This helps them learn new things, but it also helps them to accept themselves for who they are instead of constantly trying to change themselves. They will have a greater chance of future success because they will be able to take care of themselves and work at their own pace without being concerned with what others think. Knowing everyone is different is also important because it helps children respect others as individuals and avoid stereotyping those around them.

9. Self-sufficiency

Children with secure attachments are far more likely to be self-sufficient than those who do not have such high levels of security. These children tend to be able to take care of themselves. They are less likely to need a lot of help from others and can take care of many of their own needs.

These will be more likely to resist giving in and relying on others when faced with a problem because they know they can solve it independently if necessary. In the future, these people will have a greater sense of independence and understand that they only need to rely on others for things that cannot be done by themselves.

10. Increased Life Satisfaction

Children with strong attachment figures have higher levels of life satisfaction than those without secure attachments. They are less likely to be discouraged when faced with problems in life and more likely to accept others as they are. This makes them happier in general, and the two work together to make these children more successful in life. Secure attachment helps these children learn how to regulate their emotions and experiences to be happy with what they have. They also tend to be more self-sufficient, giving them more resources for being happy in life.

These people are less likely to give up or become overly demanding when faced with problems because they know they can take care of themselves. However, because they are aware that people care about them and want them to succeed, they will also be more prone to seek assistance when necessary.

In the future, these children will be more capable of happiness and delight than people who lack stable bonds. They tend to act out less because they know that someone is there for them if something goes wrong. When these children are older, this increased happiness may also make them healthier because of how happy and satisfied they are with life.

11. Greater Emotional Awareness

Children with secure attachments have greater emotional awareness than those without such strong attachment levels. When issues arise, these children are more likely to seek help from others instead of running away from the problem. They are also less likely to be fearful or angry when faced with problems because they know that someone else will help them. They are also more likely to try and find a solution to the problem rather than give up or act out violently. They know there is no point in hating or blaming others.

12. Empathy

Children with secure attachments are significantly more empathetic than those without such strong attachments. They will be more willing to comfort someone who is hurt or upset, even when it is not easy for them to do so. Secure attachment helps kids learn how to feel what others feel, allowing them to care about others. They will also be less likely to get frustrated when things do not go their way.

A secure attachment with a caregiver or parent is the best way to raise a happy, well-adjusted child. Secure attachments help children develop several positive traits that will benefit them throughout life.

CHAPTER 2

WHAT IS DISMISSIVE AVOIDANT ATTACHMENT?

Dismissive avoidant attachment (is a term for someone who tries to avoid emotional connections with others. This attachment style can influence how individuals develop intimate relationships and the amount of emotional support they receive from others.

Characteristics of Someone With Dismissive Avoidant Attachment

To understand the qualities of dismissive avoidant attachment, one must understand the characteristics that make up the dismissive avoidant attachment style – which are:

1. Self-absorbed

The main theme in dismissive avoidant attachment stems from a core belief that one's self-worth is not dependent on the existence of others. This means they will view others as unnecessary and that they only exist to fulfill their needs or help them achieve something they want.

The following behaviors result from the person's self-absorption:

a. Protects Their Identity

The dismissive avoidant will always try to protect their identity because they believe that others are not needed for them to be happy or well-adjusted. They will try not to get close to anyone else because they only want to rely on themselves. If anyone tries to befriend them, they will likely push them away because they fear that the person will hurt or betray them.

b. Independence

Dismissive avoidants believe that others are unnecessary in their lives and only exist to fulfill their needs or wants, so they will try and become independent from others. This is a way to protect themselves from getting hurt. They only trust themselves and would rather be alone than risk getting close with someone else and then having their trust in this person destroyed by betrayal. Being independent also prevents others from seeing how vulnerable they really are.

They will do all they can to make sure no one knows them on an emotional level. This means they will do whatever it takes to avoid emotional connections with others. This is why these people often have strong tendencies toward narcissism. They attempt to conceal their true self and identity from others, as they want everyone to hold them in high regard.

2. Seeks Little Support

The dismissive avoidant often believes the do no need much support. In other words, these people are self-sufficient and do not do things for others unless it benefits them or helps them achieve something they want.

The following are a few examples of this kind of person:

a. Will Put Themselves First

The dismissive avoidant will do more for themselves than others because they believe others are not needed in order to be happy or well-adjusted; therefore it is only natural for them to put their needs first. They will do things for the people close to them only if it benefits them somehow. This could be anything – material, financial, or romantic.

b. Not Allergic to Attention

The dismissive avoidant does not mind getting a little attention. They are usually very involved in their own life and may have difficulty opening up to others. They will often spend time with people just to get the attention that they need to stop feeling insecure or unhappy about themselves. They rely on attention more than others do for happiness or self-worth.

c. Can Hide Their Vulnerability

Dismissive avoidants will find ways to hide their vulnerability, so others do not see it. They live their life trying to build barriers so no one else can cause them any harm or pain. These walls they build are created to protect themselves from getting hurt by someone else.

If people get close to this kind of person, they will eventually see how vulnerable they are in certain situations. For example, they may be too scared to get close to their lovers because they think they may abuse or leave them because of something that happened in the past.

d. Negative Thinking

Dismissive avoidants do not always have a positive approach to life. They will lead a practical and realistic life but may not be overly optimistic. This means they will not always see the brighter side of things or stay upbeat.

They are also likely to ruminate about one thing for too long. When they do find a positive aspect in something that has happened, it will only last for a short period until they go back to thinking negatively again.

3. Hides Emotions

Because they are reluctant to reveal their true emotions to others, the dismissive avoidant will not always express themselves when they are upset. They will hide their emotions to protect themselves from getting hurt and may act like everything is okay when it is not. They will often hide their emotions until they are alone and then try to figure out why they feel the way they do.

The following are ways in which they hide their emotions:

a. Do Not Always Communicate with Others

They want to protect themselves from harm because they are concerned about how others might react if they express their feelings. They might feel more at ease speaking with someone who is not particularly close to them.

They try to avoid caring about others because they are afraid to hurt someone and do not have the strength to let them know how they feel. They do not want anyone to know that they are hurting.

b. Do Not Always Get Emotional

Even if a person says something that is upsetting, the dismissive avoidant will not show much of an emotional reaction to what has been said. This could be because they are trying to hide the fact that they are hurt and feeling vulnerable by making themselves seem strong. They will often bottle up their emotions until they have time alone to understand why these feelings have come up.

c. Do Not Always Show Emotion on Their Face

Even if a person has hurt them and this person is in their line of sight, the dismissive avoidant will not show that they are feeling upset. This is because they do not want to show others they are hurt or sad. After all, they do not feel like it is necessary. They do not want people to think that this person means enough to them to get mad, or that they care about what was said.

4. Suspiciousness

The dismissive avoidant tends to be suspicious because they are often very cautious. They have this tendency because they are very protective of themselves and do not want anyone to see their weaknesses.

The following are some of the ways that a dismissive avoidant can be suspicious:

a. Suspecting Someone of Deceiving Them

It can be difficult for them to believe that another person cares about them, so they may have trouble believing others have good intentions when they say something or treat them a certain way. They may also need proof of what someone is saying or doing. All of this can lead to a distrusting nature.

b. Lack of Trust

They may find it difficult to believe that the other person is being sincere. They will not trust this person and may think that they do not care about them.

c. Do Not Always Understand Why Someone Does Something Nice for Others

Sometimes a person can do something nice for them, but they will not show gratitude for what this person did for them. They may think that this person is trying to manipulate or use them in some way.

They may not appreciate why some things done for them because they do not understand why this person cares about them or why they are nice to them. They will not trust anyone who tries to show that they care about another person or help them in any way.

5. Tries to Avoid Conflict

This type of person does not enjoy conflict as it can cause a lot of tension and hurt feelings. They avoid conflict whenever possible.

The following are some reasons why the dismissive avoidant may try to avoid conflict:

a. Confrontations Are More Emotional for Them

The dismissive avoidant can be very emotional and dramatic when it comes to these confrontations, which is why they try to avoid them altogether. They do not like these interactions because they can end up feeling very hurt and ridiculed. The dismissive avoidant will rarely go through a confrontation because it tends to be more emotional for them when it does happen.

b. Likes to Think Things Through to Avoid Confrontation

Instead of confronting someone if they have a problem or issue with them, they may wait and see if it will go away or if the other person will address this issue. They do not want to talk about things because the conflict can be too much for them to handle.

If someone starts something with them, they may try to get out of this interaction as soon as possible, so they do not have to hear the other person's side of what happened.

c. Feels Conflicted Because They Want to Confront Someone About Something, But They Also Want to Avoid The Situation

The dismissive avoidant may try to fix the problem without confrontation because they believe it will cause more tension and conflict for them. They will choose their battles wisely so that there are no confrontations involved.

Avoiding conflicts is one of the main reasons that the dismissive avoidant is seen as not caring about anyone. They do not enjoy these confrontations, and it causes a lot of tension. It can also hurt their feelings and make them feel very scared and vulnerable.

6. Low Self-esteem

This type of person generally does not think they can do things well. They do not believe that they are capable of achieving their goals. This can cause many complications in their life because they do not trust themselves or have the confidence to strive for success.

The following are some ways that the dismissive avoidant exhibits low self-esteem:

a. Doubts Themselves and Their Abilities

When the dismissive avoidant gets involved with other people, they may doubt themselves and their abilities. This person does not feel like others see them as a strong individual because of how much criticism is given to them throughout the day. They don't think they'll ever succeed in their endeavors or get where they want to go, and this can make them frustrated and demoralized. They need to learn that they are a strong individual and capable of performing in many different situations, or they may continue to have problems with their self-esteem.

b. Focus On How Others See Them

The dismissive avoidant may become very focused on what others are saying about them or how other people perceive them. They may think other people are always judging or saying bad things about them. The dismissive avoidant may become overly preoccupied with what other people think or say about them because they don't feel in control of the situation. This can cause them to seek help from others who they perceive to be more successful than they are. They might consult these people for advice, but if the advice is bad or the advisor is incompetent, this could lead to even more problems.

c. Feel That They Are Being Judged by Others Constantly

When the dismissive avoidant is around others, it is possible for them to feel like other people are constantly judging them. They may think that other people are always saying negative things about them, which can cause them to become very insecure and upset. This causes a lot of pain and frustration and cause them to become upset instead of happy when a new day begins.

The low self-esteem of the dismissive avoidant can cause them to have problems in their life that they need to overcome. This type of person will not feel capable of achieving their goals or doing well in their everyday journeys. They need to avoid letting other people's opinions affect them too much because this may cause them to lose confidence.

CHAPTER 3

WHAT CAUSES DISMISSIVE AVOIDANT ATTACHMENT?

A child's attachment style is formed by how they interact with their parents while growing up. This does not imply that dismissive avoidant attachment does not occur later in life. Still, the patterns developed in the earlier years will likely remain throughout an individual's life. Below are several of the factors that can contribute to a dismissive avoidant attachment style:

Genetics

In most cases, genetics will play a significant role in determining an individual's attachment style. If a person's parents have a dismissive avoidant attachment, they have a high chance of developing the same attachment style.

The following genes play a part in creating a dismissive avoidant attachment:

a. Oxytocin Receptor Gene (OXTR)

The OXTR gene is one of the oxytocin receptors responsible for regulating how we bond (i.e., affection, trust, etc.) with others. Those who have at least one defective OXTR gene are more likely to develop a dismissive avoidant attachment, especially if one or both of their parents has the same attachment style. Such individuals will likely have difficulty forming emotional bonds with others, which may lead to emotional distance from their romantic partner(s) and their children.

b. Dopamine Receptor Genes (DRD4 and DRD2)

Norepinephrine, epinephrine, and dopamine are three neurotransmitters that play an important role in regulating our moods. Those with defective dopamine receptors tend to be more aggressive, angry, and temperamental than those without a defect in this receptor. The same can be said for norepinephrine levels. Those with a defective gene for norepinephrine tend to be more impulsive, obsessive-compulsive, and unstable than those not deficient in this gene.

People with high dopamine levels tend to be calm and composed, whereas those with low dopamine levels are more prone to agitation and aggression. Those with low dopamine are more likely to become angry or irritable in new or stressful situations. This is probably because their bodies become flooded with an excess amount of norepinephrine (i.e., fight-or-flight response) which results in their cortisol levels rising and their blood pressure and heart rate going up. Thus they become more agitated, confused, and upset.

c. 5HT2A Receptor Genes

5HT2A, also known as the serotonin receptor type 2A, regulates our mood and social behavior. Individuals with a defective 5HT2A gene frequently display impulsive and agitated behavior, which increases their risk of developing a dismissive avoidant attachment, particularly if one or both of their parents exhibit these traits.

Due to a possible defect in their 5HT2A genes, those who have inherited this gene are likely to experience distress and agitation when interacting with their family members. According to attachment theory, this behavior is usually motivated by the need for safety and security. Because they become distressed by being around those they love, it can be assumed that they might have experienced abuse or neglect from the people they trust (i.e., family). Due to these experiences, many of these people have a tendency to dismiss and avoid others as a means of self-defense when they worry about being despised and abandoned by others. Their relationships become more important as they rely on others for safety and security.

d. D4DR Gene (Also Known as "the Novelty-seeking Gene")

Researchers say that the D4DR gene significantly determines our ability to adapt to new things and environments. However, those with a defective D4DR gene are more likely to develop a dismissive avoidant attachment because they may not be able to engage with others as easily as their peers.

The novelty-seeking gene is inherited from both parents and is responsible for how we interact with new environments (i.e., situations that have never been experienced before). Thus, as this gene influences our ability to adapt to new situations, it is highly likely that those who inherit a defective version of this gene will experience greater difficulty or stress when interacting with others than those without the defect. For example, those who inherit a defective D4DR gene may experience stress and anxiety when entering into relationships with new people due to their inability to adapt to the new environment. They may then find it more difficult to develop emotional connections with others and open up to potential romantic interests or family members. Meanwhile, those who inherit a non-defective version of this gene can easily adapt to changing circumstances, which makes it easier for them to form emotional bonds with others and become available to their loved ones.

e. Alpha-2A Adrenergic Receptor Gene

The alpha-2A adrenergic receptor (α2AR) is responsible for regulating blood pressure and heartbeat. It accomplishes this by either enhancing or impairing these essential bodily processes. Those with a defective α2AR gene are more likely to have an overly sensitive fight-or-flight response and react faster than those without this defect, making it more difficult for these individuals to become available to family members because they are often very agitated and stressed when interacting with them.

Those who inherit a defective α2AR gene can become easily agitated and anxious when interacting with others, especially with family members. As a result, many of these individuals prefer being alone to spending time with others (i.e., family), which can give rise to a dismissive avoidant attachment style.

Genes are correlated with the way that we respond to certain stimuli. They are also related to our personality, age, how we interact with others, and our evolution and personality. According to attachment theory, genes pass down information to us through our DNA (deoxyribonucleic acid). Thus it is important to know that if you have a family history of a particular trait or behavioral pattern (e.g., avoidant attachment), there is a chance that you may inherit the trait or pattern from your parents.

Environment

Our environment has a strong impact on whether an individual is likely to develop a dismissive avoidant attachment.

Three main environmental factors can lead to the development of a dismissive avoidant attachment:

a. Family Background & Social Class

Social class is a significant factor in dismissive avoidant attachment, particularly when the parents are of different social classes.

Sociological studies have shown that lower-social-class or status individuals are at greater risk of suffering from a dismissive avoidant attachment than higher-status individuals. This is because parents from lower-class or poor backgrounds often lack the social skills to engage with others. After all, they were often never taught how to communicate effectively and handle relationships owing to their upbringing and the fact that they were not exposed to many social interactions that could have improved their communication skills. As a result, these parents may not always be available or responsive to their children's needs and desires.

In contrast, parents from a higher social class or wealthy background are usually more capable of engaging with others owing to their greater communication skills, which they learned while growing up and interacting with others. As a result, these parents can be more available and supportive of their children when they need them, foster a greater level of emotional security in the child, engage more effectively with others in general, and are more likely to show consistent levels of affection toward their children. It is much easier for these children to form emotional bonds with their parents as they can easily access their help and assistance, further developing a trusting relationship between them.

b. Cultural Factors

In addition to social class, culture is another factor leading to a dismissive avoidant attachment. Specifically, a child's cultural background influences their view of and interaction with others. In some cultures, children are discouraged from interacting with others from different cultures as they may be less likely to trust or form an attachment to them. This is especially true if the developing child's parents believe their culture is superior. Children exposed to only one particular culture may develop negative views about those who belong to other cultures as they grow older.

James Coleman, a social psychologist, claims that the nature vs. nurture controversy is a crucial application of his theory of cultural influence. According to Coleman, culture is "a set of socially-shared values, beliefs, and practices transmitted from one generation to the next using directly or indirectly imitating behavior." Therefore it seems that our parents' values strongly influence us throughout our lives, which may influence our behavior.

Cultures vary greatly from region to region. As a result, values, beliefs, and practices also differ greatly within each region. Certain cultures may have high expectations around child-rearing or a high need for communication by parents with their children compared to other cultures. As a result, these two cultures may differ in the attention they give their children while they are growing up. In turn, this may affect how a child forms an emotional bond with their parents as they may only interact with them when they are out of the house and not during their daily activities. Some people may even have different standards of friendship than those who live in their own country due to cultural differences. For example, in America, people generally have a higher standard of friendship than they do in China or Japan, where people may be less emotionally invested in forming close friends. As a result, Americans are much more likely to develop a secure attachment style than Chinese or Japanese people, who generally cannot handle close relationships.

c. Life Experiences

The life experiences of a child, particularly their level of exposure to negative and traumatic experiences, are also key factors in developing an avoidant attachment style.

The following is a list of traumatic experiences that may lead to the development of a dismissive avoidant attachment:

a. Child Sexual Abuse

Child sexual abuse or molestation is one of the most significant causes of dismissive avoidant attachment.

Child molestation involves unwanted and inappropriate sexual contact between an adult and child. It can cause great emotional pain for both the child and the adult perpetrator. The adult may not only sexualize their relationship with their children such that they are not treated as people but instead as objects for sexual use, but may also try to convince the child that it is their fault or that they instigated it. This can significantly impact a child's self-concept and their relationship with their family.

Often incestual abuse occurs within households among parents and children or siblings who live with one another. When a close relative commits the crime, they may use guilt and manipulation to make the victimized child believe they are at least partially to blame. This can have a serious impact on their mental health.

b. Institutionalized Child Abuse

Children who are exposed to alcohol abuse, neglect, or physical and sexual violence are at the mercy of those they should be able to trust the most, and these experiences frequently cause children to develop an avoidant attachment style. It is especially common for those who live in orphanages or institutions to develop this style because they have no to relate during their formative years. They develop a deep mistrust of others, particularly men in positions of authority. In addition, the person who is supposed to be the child's caregiver may make them feel it is their fault for being abused or neglected and fail to provide a safe environment for the child.

c. Loss of a Parent

Loss of a parent or guardian is one of the children's most significant causes of dismissive avoidant attachment. It can cause major upheaval in a child's life, especially if they feel they must take on the caretaker role.

d. Divorce and Separation

Divorce and separation are traumatic events that often lead to a breakdown of the parent-child relationship, partly because a child may feel as though they must be "all grown up" to get their parent's attention and that their existence does not make much of a difference to the world. This might be especially true for younger kids who don't have the coping mechanisms to deal with parental divorce. They may also develop a deep sense of shame or guilt at having been involved in such a family crisis, leading them to suppress all memories associated with this period and view themselves as bad and unworthy. This can create a sense of detachment from their parents and family members who, because of the divorce or separation, may be too distracted to pay attention to their child. This can damage the parent-child relationship and can lead to the child developing a dismissive avoidant attachment style.

A child may develop a dismissive avoidant attachment style if they are overwhelmed by the loss of a parent and have no other family members to whom they can relate, especially if they are raised in an orphanage or institution or are living independently for the first time. If a child raised by divorced parents does not have an older sibling to help them navigate this new situation, they must find ways to deal with their overwhelming emotions about the loss of their parent alone. This can interfere with their secure attachment style because they may feel as though they have no one to fall back on in times of need. They learn that expressing emotion can lead to abandonment, which can lead to an avoidant attachment style.

e. Unfavorable Life Events

Unfavorable life circumstances such as natural disasters and war are partly responsible for the growing number of people with the dismissive avoidant attachment type in modern times. The aftermath of these events, especially when it involves large groups being wiped out by a disaster, can cause people to feel helpless and abandoned. This creates a sense of vulnerability. Because the traumatized people in their society have lost hope, they tend to become dismissive-avoidant and view themselves as bad or worthless people who are not worth caring about. This leads them to feel out of control and fearful that they may face similar, if not worse, misfortune in the future. They may also feel rejected by their government if it is the cause of their misfortune, which leaves them feeling unworthy and abandoned.

Your life circumstances and personal history can greatly impact the development of your attachment style.

Other Factors

There are other factors which can cause someone to develop a dismissive avoidant attachment style.

1. Mental Disorders

Mental disorders can lead to a dismissive dismissive-avoidant attachment style. These include:

a. Borderline Personality Disorder

A dismissive-avoidant attachment style can emerge in people with borderline personality disorder (BPD). While some people with BPD lack clear boundaries and cannot set healthy limits with good communication, others can carefully articulate their boundaries as long as they feel safe. However, they tend to have difficulty setting healthy boundaries when frightened or threatened. Because they may feel hopeless and helpless when unable to control their emotions, they may develop an avoidant attachment style out of fear of abandonment. This is particularly true if they had a parent who was emotionally unavailable, punishing in the face of their emotions, or who was frequently preoccupied with their own issues.

In addition, people with BPD often feel as though they are misunderstood, partly due to their inability to articulate their feelings accurately. However, it has also been demonstrated that many people have the wrong impression of them because their actions are typically viewed as manipulative. Because of this, they may be afraid that they will not be taken seriously if they try to communicate their needs and fears, leading them to develop an avoidant style.

According to a study by Shaver and Hazan, 98% of people with BPD have a dismissive avoidant attachment style. This is partly because their sense of self is negatively affected by their inability to control their emotions, negatively impacting how they view others. Because they have not learned to acknowledge their needs and ask for what they want and need, they do not expect others to help them. Further, they view those aware of their wants as making unreasonable demands that cannot be met. This leads them to believe that others will reject them if they try to get what they want, promoting a dismissive-avoidant attachment style.

b. ADHD/ADD

Attention deficit hyperactivity disorder (ADHD) and attention deficit disorder (ADD), which include the symptoms of inattention and impulsivity, can influence how a child grows up and forms an attachment style. In children with ADHD, the lack of ability to manage their emotions can make it difficult for them to regulate their behavior. When they feel out of control, they may develop a dismissive-avoidant attachment style. This is especially true if excessively controlling, and punitive parents raised them.

While growing up, these children may have been told to be more 'still' or quiet because their behavior disrupted the household. Because of this, they learned that if they felt something inside of them and wanted to express it, others would see them as being out of control and unsafe enough to trust. They may also have felt they were not being taken seriously, especially when they were told that their emotions were 'no big deal' or that they would grow out of them. In addition, others may have viewed their expression of emotion as a sign of disrespect and punished them for it, causing them to feel like their feelings are wrong and that it is not okay to show them. This can leave them angry, frustrated, and afraid because they know that their behavior upsets others. Because of this, they may decide to avoid expressing themselves by developing an avoidant attachment style to be left alone by those who do not seem to understand them.

While some with ADHD seek out relationships where they feel special by being the center of attention, others develop a dismissive-avoidant style to protect themselves from the discomfort of feeling rejected or abandoned. This is because those with ADHD can have difficulty regulating themselves. They have difficulty staying focused on one task because their minds often wander to consider other fun or challenging things. This is particularly true in social settings where excitement and unpredictability are expected, making them feel as though their attachment needs may not be met if they do not behave in a way that is consistent with others. Because of this, they may fear that others will not understand them if they do not respond similarly. This can make them feel that their reactions are inappropriate, especially when they have an overwhelming sense of frustration or sadness.

c. Anorexia Nervosa

People with anorexia nervosa can develop a dismissive-avoidant attachment style because of how their illness makes them feel about themselves. Individuals with anorexia may believe that they are not good enough or that something is wrong with them, although the effects can vary. As a result, they often do not believe others will like them if they know the truth about them. In addition, it may be difficult for others to understand their behavior, leaving them distrustful.

This can lead those with anorexia to develop a dismissive-avoidant attachment style because they are afraid that others will not support them if they disclose their thoughts or feelings about their body or life. This is especially true if they are from an unstable or inconsistent family environment, which makes it difficult for them to rely on their parent or caretaker for support and comfort. While they were trying to manage their food and eating behaviors, they may have been criticized or shamed by others in their household. As a result, their attachment style is dismissive-avoidant because they fear that the people around them will abandon them if they reveal too much about themselves, and they need time alone or alone with no one else around to buffer the feelings overwhelming them.

d. Obsessive Compulsive Disorder (OCD)

People with OCD often have a dismissive-avoidant attachment style because they avoid people they feel will not understand them. In addition, it may be hard for them to find someone with the patience and understanding required to provide the support they need. They may develop a dismissive-avoidant attachment style to avoid rejection by those closest to them.

According to research by *The Journal of Abnormal Psychology*, dismissive-avoidant attachment styles are more prevalent in OCD sufferers. They may feel uncomfortable or even afraid when asked to express their thoughts and feelings straightforwardly. In response, they become more reclusive and defensive.

e. Post-traumatic Stress Disorder (PTSD)

Because of how it makes them feel about themselves and others, post-traumatic stress disorder (PTSD) can lead to the development of a dismissive-avoidant attachment style. Many individuals with PTSD have difficulty trusting others because they have been abandoned by those who should have supported them. This can result from being in an abusive relationship or feeling as though the people around them do not validate their emotions, thoughts, and feelings. As a result, many people with PTSD avoid getting close to the people around them, making it difficult for others to connect with them.

According to a study by an article in *The Journal of Nervous & Mental Disease*, some individuals may show signs of PTSD early on in life, before any traumatic experience that could explain their symptoms. These individuals often have a dismissive-avoidant attachment style, making it difficult for a clinician to suggest the best treatment. They might feel embarrassed or unable to discuss their illness.

People with PTSD tend to separate from others because they feel they are not being taken seriously by the people around them. Many PTSD sufferers find it difficult to fully trust others, which makes them distance themselves from those closest to them. They worry that if they reveal too much about themselves, others will reject them.

A mental disorder can significantly increase your chance of having a dismissive-avoidant attachment style. This is because it can cause you to feel as though you need to be alone or close yourself off from others to protect yourself from rejection or abandonment.

2. Physical Health Impairment

Physical health impairments can increase your risk of developing a dismissive-avoidant attachment style. Such impairments can include the following:

a. Chronic Pain

Chronic pain can make it difficult for you to be fully receptive to others and manage your own life. Because chronic pain makes it difficult for you to maintain close relationships with other people, it may lead to a dismissive-avoidant attachment style.

Chronic pain can make it difficult for people to form close relationships with others. They may also find it difficult to consider other people's feelings and needs, which can lead them to become frustrated or angry with those closest to them. As a result, the kind of support they need and want from others is less likely to be obtained. Due to their discomfort with fully revealing themselves, they may also lose interest in activities that call for social interaction, which makes it challenging for them to participate fully in worthwhile experiences.

They tend to distance themselves from others because they feel their pain is not taken seriously by those around them. In addition, they may experience fear toward expressing how they feel about other people and their needs because they believe that no one will care about them or support them. Due to all of these emotions, many people with chronic pain may end up becoming more aloof and resistant to the people around them.

b. Prolonged Illnesses

Prolonged illnesses, such as cancer and AIDS, can also impact a person's ability to be receptive to others.

In many cases, the distress caused by a prolonged illness can lead to a dismissive-avoidant attachment style. This is because these illnesses frequently result in depressive or anxious symptoms, which can lead a person to isolate themselves from other people out of fear of being rejected or abandoned.

A prolonged illness can make it difficult for you to meet your needs and wants, which can cause a person to become more closed off from others. As a result, these people might start to believe they are alone and have no one to turn to. This, in turn, can make them more guarded, making it challenging for them to trust others fully.

Many individuals with chronic illnesses may also feel as though they do not have the energy to continue strengthening their relationships with those around them, making it difficult for them to maintain close relationships.

c. Injury

Certain types of injuries, such as brain damage or spinal cord injuries, can also increase your chance of having a dismissive-avoidant attachment style. These injuries can limit a person's ability to interact with others and participate fully in relationships. As a result, an individual may become more closed off from others and develop a dismissive-avoidant attachment style.

After a trauma or injury, the survivor must re-evaluate their close relationships and make changes to continue living a productive life. This can affect their ability to maintain relationships.

The loss of ability caused by some injuries can cause a person to become closed off from others and more self-focused. They become more protective of themselves, which can lead to a dismissive-avoidant attachment style.

Pain or trauma caused by physical illnesses, injury, or prolonged health problems can trigger an attachment disorder and increase the chance of having a dismissive-avoidant attachment style. People's responses to these issues may change their ability to get close to others and affect their attachment style. Concerns about how others respond to them, their inability to meet their own needs and wants, and the changes caused by physical pain or trauma can all lead a person to be more closed off from others and form a dismissive-avoidant attachment style.

3. Everyday Activities

Things you do in everyday life can also lead to an increased chance of having a dismissive-avoidant attachment style. These include:

a. Drug Abuse

Drugs alter a person's mood, perceptions, or consciousness. Substances such as cocaine and heroin can be addictive and can affect how someone feels about themselves and others. The mood changes caused by these substances tend to cause certain individuals to become defensive and unresponsive to their environment. This may cause them to develop a dismissive-avoidant attachment style.

In many cases, those who abuse drugs often feel they are not good enough or do not deserve the love of the people around them. This can cause them to withdraw from their surroundings. As a result, they may have trouble forming close relationships and instead form a dismissive-avoidant attachment style. In addition, many people with these issues often express themselves in ways others do not understand, and they may be more difficult to get close to.

According to the National Institute on Drug Abuse, drug addiction is a chronic disease. This means that it does not go away by itself; instead, it requires ongoing treatment for the rest of one's life. According to the NIDA, about 10% of people who begin using drugs will become dependent on them. People with an attachment disorder can get into a coping mechanism or pattern that causes them to abuse drugs or alcohol to cope with the problems and challenges they face in daily life.

b. Alcohol Abuse

Alcohol is a substance that alters a person's mood, perceptions, or consciousness. Alcohol abuse can lead to some people feeling as though they are not good enough or do not deserve the love of the people around them. Sometimes, these feelings make people withdraw from their surroundings. This may cause people who have an alcohol abuse issue to form a dismissive-avoidant attachment style.

Individuals with alcoholism issues may experience intense shame and humiliation. Furthermore, these individuals can feel intimidated or panic when someone expects them to follow through on their responsibilities in society or the community at large. They may also have trouble making reasonable decisions and solving problems. This leads to an increased chance of having a dismissive-avoidant attachment style.

c. Stress

Stress is anxiety or emotional turmoil arising from a conflict in your life that you do not feel prepared to deal with. About 47.4% of adults reported experiencing significant stress in their daily lives, according to the Anxiety and Depression Association of America. This means that about one-third or 34% of adults in the United States experience debilitating stress levels at least once a week. Anxiety disorder sufferers are more likely to have a dismissive-avoidant attachment style than the general population.

Those with an anxiety disorder are likely to experience bouts of intense anxiety when they cannot fulfill their needs for love, attention, and security from the people around them. Furthermore, they may have difficulty controlling their feelings of panic and fear because they may have trouble turning their feelings off or avoiding situations that make them anxious. This can cause them to have trouble making reasonable decisions and solving problems.

d. Relationship Problems

Problems can arise in any relationship. Sometimes, these relationship problems can contribute to a person developing a dismissive-avoidant attachment style.

According to the University of Texas Health Science Center Medical School, relationship problems affect about one-third or 34% of adults in the United States at least once a week. In addition, about 16% experience relationship problems that cause them to feel extremely upset or distressed every day. This means that people who experience relationship problems may be more likely to have trouble responding to the needs of others because they are too preoccupied with their own problems and concerns. They may also have trouble making reasonable decisions and solving problems. This can lead to an increased chance of a dismissive-avoidant attachment style.

e. Job Problems

Job problems are a slightly more specific form of relationship problems, and can sometimes cause people to develop dismissive-avoidant attachment styles. People who experience job problems in their lives may have trouble responding to the needs of others because they are too preoccupied with their own problems and concerns. They may also have trouble making reasonable decisions and solving problems, which can lead to a dismissive-avoidant attachment style.

There are a lot of things that can cause someone to have a dismissive-avoidant attachment style. However, someone with a dismissive-avoidant attachment style can still have a good quality of life. People are never too old or broken to get help.

PART 2

DISMISSIVE AVOIDATNS IN RELATIONSHIPS

CHAPTER 4

HOW DISMISSIVE AVOIDANTS LOVE

Falling in love is different for every one of us. It's a feeling that usually hits us unexpectedly, but at the same time, it can be as simple as that feeling when you put on a pair of pants for the first time and it feels like they were made just for you. Falling in love is something we all experience in our lives, whether it's with someone we know or a person we meet by chance. For almost everyone, this love will turn into a relationship.

Despite their attachment style, dismissive-avoidants are capable of having a relationship with someone they love and feel passionate about. As love is a complex emotion and has many definitions, the love shown by someone with a dismissive-avoidant attachment may differ from that of someone with a secure attachment. How the person with dismissive-avoidant attachment looks at love is unique to their own experience.

What Does Love Look Like?

The qualities that characterize love are understood by everyone who has ever been in a relationship. Some of these qualities are demonstrated by kind and compassionate actions, such as the agreement to assist one another through good and difficult times, as well as through dedication or sacrifice. Other characteristics require an expression of emotions, such as lust or jealousy. Some people in relationships may feel that their love is not strong enough, despite having an emotional reaction, such as lust or jealousy, to something their partner did. This is the difference between someone with secure attachment and a person with dismissive-avoidant attachment.

Characteristics of Dismissive-avoidants in a Relationship

The following characteristics are typically associated with someone with a dismissive-avoidant attachment style. They are not always present in every dismissive-avoidant, but they will be present more often than not.

1. Tendency to feel lukewarm about commitment

People with this attachment style are less likely to respond well when their partner wants a more serious relationship. They often desire to go out and experience new things without their partner and tend to feel that if they settle down with their current partner, other relationships would seem much more appealing.

They will do the following things:

a. Not being able to commit fully to the relationship

Dismissive-avoidants will be more likely to have unrealistic ideas about what love is and what a committed relationship looks like. When their partner starts talking about wanting to spend more time together, pursuing a dream of marriage and children, or even establishing a business together, their dismissive-avoidant partner becomes less happy. This is because they are not looking for a partner who will spend a lot of time with them or with who they can build something with; instead, they are looking for someone to be their companion, not necessarily someone to share their dreams and goals with. Even once the dismissive avoidant has found a partner with which they are comfortable spending time, it's hard for them to let their guard down fully and be completely committed.

The dismissive avoidant will have difficulties becoming emotionally attached to their partner. The two of them will often grow apart, leaving the dismissive avoidant feeling less happy and that something is wrong with their love life. Once they get over this phase, however, they enjoy the freedom of being single.

b. They believe commitment will limit their options

A person with this attachment style is more likely to look for reasons why a relationship will not work out rather than why it could work out. This presents itself through fantasizing about alternative partners and how things could be better with someone else. The dismissive avoidant will also feel threatened when their partner wants to be in a committed relationship or wants to talk or show love in a way that is too strong. They will feel like they are being pushed into something they don't want to do and cannot express what is on their mind.

In relationships, when the dismissive avoidant does commit to a relationship, they will usually get bored quickly. This can be because they don't feel like their partner is affectionate or romantic enough or because the relationship seems too boring. They like new things and experiences, so they will start to resent that they are with the same person all the time. This makes them less invested in their partner and more likely to cheat on them or look for other partners.

c. Tendency to fantasize about alternative partners

They will often be attracted to people with the same attachment style. When they go out with their partner, they may think about how much better things were when they were single. They can easily become more interested in someone else who seems exciting. This is when the dismissive avoidant will start to justify cheating or breaking up with their partner. They tend to be secretly unhappy and unfulfilled most of the time, even though no one can tell that anything is wrong.

Dismissive avoidants can be very good at hiding their true feelings and thoughts about a relationship, and because of this, the person they are with may never really know what is going on in their mind. This can lead them to believe that the dismissive avoidant doesn't care about them as much as they do when the dismissive avoidant is just unsure of how they feel.

d. Can be overly critical of their partner

They feel like they know what is best for their partner and themselves because they have an unrealistic idea of love. They may be controlling with their spouse in an effort to save themselves from getting wounded by them. They will tend to distance themselves from their partner because they don't want to get too close to someone who might reject them later. This is where the criticism comes in. It's not that the dismissive avoidant doesn't care about their partner; it's just that it's hard for them to express their feelings.

e. Tendency to feel lonely but be uncomfortable with too much closeness

They fear that they will be rejected and abandoned, which comes from past experiences in their life. This fear of rejection is something they have to learn how to overcome when being in a relationship. Because they are concerned that their partner will reject them and leave them behind if they let their guard down, the dismissive avoidant may frequently push their lover away or not fully commit to them. They do this because of their bad past relationships and feelings about love. Many dismissive avoidants will feel lonely because they aren't in a relationship and then feel like something is wrong with them because they don't have someone in their life to share things with.

This can be frustrating for a partner who wants to be more supportive of the dismissive avoidant who does not want to open up. This can sometimes lead to arguments. The dismissive avoidant may feel like there is nothing to talk about when they are really afraid of what they may say, or they will avoid talking about things that are making them feel bad or upset.

Commitment for someone with dismissive-avoidant attachment is no easy task. They take time to build trust in a relationship and have a propensity to "draw away" emotionally when they sense their spouse wants them to be even more attached or devoted. This is a defense mechanism against being hurt. Thus it is natural for someone with this attachment style to do so. The dismissive-avoidant's fear of abandonment causes the cycle of fear and pushing away their partner. Eventually, their partner will feel hurt and want out, leaving the dismissive avoidant feeling abandoned once again, reinforcing the cycle they are used to experiencing from childhood.

2. Likely to not see themselves as "in love."

Dismissive avoidants are usually going through some level of confusion in their life, and they can often be unaware of it.

This kind of relationship can be confusing for everyone involved. The partner and the dismissive avoidant may feel hurt, rejected, and unhappy most of the time because the relationship lacks the connection many people desire in a committed relationship.

They will do the following things:

a. Their focus is usually on what they think a relationship should be like

Because they are so focused on what they think a relationship should be like, it is easy for them to feel their partner isn't right for them since their expectations are so high. The way they define "love" and "a romantic relationship" can make the dismissive avoidant feel very lonely.

b. They seek out relationships that are not very important to them

The dismissive avoidant will go through many relationships because the more committed a relationship becomes, the more uncomfortable it will become. This means that they usually find themselves only getting into relationships with people who aren't looking for a serious commitment but are instead looking for something casual and temporary.

c. They have a pattern of unhealthy relationships

The dismissive avoidant often struggles to have a healthy relationship because of their thoughts, feelings, and desires. The fear of being hurt causes them to pull away from their partner so they won't get hurt, but this leads them to feel isolated and lonely. They will even use their partner's "failure to be supportive" as an excuse, avoiding taking responsibility for the relationship's failure.

This leads them to have a pattern of relationships that have problems. The dismissive avoidant may have been hurt in the past and may be afraid of what will happen if they allow someone to get close to them again, which is why they push people away. This kind of pattern can also lead them to fear commitment, and the dismissive avoidant may choose partners who aren't interested in being committed to anyone at all, reinforcing their "fear of commitment" even more.

d. They want to feel needed, not loved

The dismissive avoidant has a hard time feeling the love in a relationship. Instead of feeling loved, they will feel like the other person is "needy" or "clingy." They may also believe that their partner's neediness is an attempt at controlling them and making them feel bad. The dismissive-avoidant will be more interested in looking for someone who doesn't have needs they have to meet instead of someone who loves them and wants to be with them because of who they are.

The dismissive-avoidant may feel confused and even apathetic because they can't understand why someone would want to spend time with them. This is because, for the dismissive avoidant, it is impossible to show their significant other love, affection, and respect if they don't believe they care about them in return.

e. They have a hard time taking responsibility in a relationship

The dismissive avoidant may start blaming their partner when things don't work out. They may tell themselves, "I'm not responsible for my partner's failure to show me any love or affection." They struggle to view the world from an alternative viewpoint.

3. Difficulty being assertive or initiating intimacy

One of the biggest characteristics of the dismissive-avoidant is that they are rarely aggressive and don't like to be around people who seek closeness and affection. They will usually avoid conversations that involve feelings and intimacy. They may also avoid confrontation with their partner by walking away or distancing themselves from the situation.

The dismissive avoidant can have difficulty expressing their needs because they believe their partner should be able to read their mind and know what they need in a relationship. They may feel disappointed, angry, or resentful if their partner isn't doing what they expect of them.

They may try to get away from this feeling by avoiding talking about it altogether.

They will do the following things:

a. Shutting down intimacy

The dismissive avoidant will often prefer to be alone. They think people who want to be around others are "clingy." The dismissive avoidant will often try to shut down all communication in their relationships. If they attempt to talk, it will often be with words that don't amount much more than: "That's why I'm single/unhappy," or "I don't know what else you want me to say." The dismissive avoidant will try to walk away from a conversation that starts with "I feel hurt, confused, angry, or jealous."

b. Creating a cycle of contempt

When their partner does initiate intimacy and communication, the dismissive avoidant may respond with upsetting comments like: "I know you're not happy in this relationship," or "I can't believe you think I'm going to take care of your emotional needs." The dismissive avoidant will use these stressful comments to create a cycle of contempt and will push their significant other away further and further. They may do this because they think that if they stop talking about it, the problems will go away naturally.

The problem with this is that by not talking about it and ignoring their partner's feelings, the relationship will become a "hot potato" that they cannot just drop, so they feel as though they might as well continue to throw it around. These kinds of comments are only self-sabotaging and will inevitably end up making their partner upset with them.

d. Creating distance from their partner and others

The dismissive avoidant may start hiding out in their room for days or even weeks if things get too intimate with their partner. They may also avoid spending time with anyone besides their family, friends, or coworkers. They may avoid the company of others by saying they have too much to do at home, or they will go out of their way to avoid talking to someone else. Alternatively, they'll choose to be around someone else instead of the person they're in a relationship with. They do not like feeling pressured by their partner, so when the pressure gets too much for them, they will try to escape it by hiding.

e. Dismissiveness toward the partner

The dismissive avoidant will often look down on their partner's thoughts and feelings and will sometimes doubt the validity of what they're saying.

Because they are more likely to forget about their partner's emotional needs, they may have less compassion for them. They'll have negative emotional reactions toward their partner's feelings, such as: "You should know better than to say something like that." These reactions are very hurtful and can lead to a lack of trust.

This difficulty in communication from dismissive avoidant results from an imbalance in self-esteem and impulsivity. As they try to avoid their emotions, they become less likely to trust their partner. The more they blame the other person for making them feel bad, the more they try to escape it by getting away from that person or evading any conversation that would make them feel like they're at fault. Emotional issues do not go away without communication, so a dismissive avoidant who tries to ignore them will only worsen the situation.

4. Overly self-conscious

Dismissive avoidants are more likely to feel worried about their image and what others think of them. They will often feel like they have to prove themselves to the world by doing something they can be proud of. They may develop a very strong sense of self-consciousness in order to impress others.

Their partner may have difficulties getting angry or expressing their feelings because the dismissive avoidant is so sensitive to criticism. This can cause many problems in the relationship because there may not be much room for expressing feelings and complaints.

They will do the following things:

a. Be unsure about what to say

Dismissive avoidants aren't typically interested in discussing their feelings or personal issues. They will be less likely to want to go out of their way to make conversation and may be confused about why their partner is trying so hard to talk with them. It may feel like the other person is being too nosy and want to know everything about them, and the dismissive avoidant will not be willing to share their feelings or even give them a straight answer.

The dismissive avoidant will often be more comfortable talking with someone they feel is not so intense and demanding. It can be difficult for them to converse with others when they feel bad about themselves because it makes them think that what they have to say isn't important or interesting. This can cause them to have difficulty thinking of things to say. Dismissive avoidants may start to feel frustrated because they cannot express their feelings to the person they are in a relationship with, but they might also get frustrated at their partner for wanting too much from them.

b. Prefer to be left alone

Being in a relationship can be very stressful for the dismissive avoidant because they are more likely to feel like their partner is trying to control them by trying to find out how they feel or are doing. They will feel vulnerable when talking about personal things and may respond by pushing the other person away. When someone has been hurt too many times, they may start to avoid relationships altogether.

Dismissive avoidants might have difficulty reading their partner's emotions and will not understand why the other person is asking so many questions or feeling so demanding about their personal information. They might also be afraid that someone will find out some personal information about them and use it against them in a way they can't control. They may try to avoid this by pretending not to care or ignoring the other person, but they may end up hurting themselves by pushing their partner farther away.

c. Tend to lie to avoid conflict

Dismissive avoidants tend to lie because they don't want anyone else to know what they are thinking or feeling. They may also tell their partner things that aren't true because they are trying to avoid being reprimanded.

d. Avoid making decisions

Dismissive avoidants will often have trouble deciding what they want because they aren't so focused on their own emotions and needs. They may be afraid that if they try to figure out what they want, they will realize that they are not happy with how things are going. This is why many will avoid making any major decisions or taking risks. They might also feel afraid of making a decision because it will mean committing to one thing instead of being able to do something else if something better comes along.

5. Tendency to doubt their partner's love for them

Dismissive avoidants tend to be more emotionally detached from their partners and challenge the authenticity of their feelings for them. They doubt the other person's love because they have their own set of issues that hold them back from feeling like their partner is real. As a result, they may believe the other person doesn't care about them or that they are shallow or only in it for sex. This could cause them question if this is a bad relationship.

They will do the following things:

a. Feel that they are not worthy of being cared about

Dismissive avoidants typically feel unworthy of the attention and care they need to be happy. Their partner might want to talk about their problems and try to help them, but the dismissive avoidant will become anxious when they try to do this, and may feel that they don't deserve the attention.

This problem tends to be more prevalent in people who were neglected during their childhood. It can also happen if people experience a lot of rejection from the relationships that they have formed in adulthood.

b. Feel guilty for getting attention

When people have mixed feelings about their own emotions, they may feel like they should not be getting attention because it is unfair to their partner. They may also think that if they talk about how they are feeling, their partner might leave them.

c. Inability to read their partner

Dismissive avoidant individuals are not good at reading other people and might not pay attention to the other person's body language and facial expressions. They may even tell the other person that they don't care about what is happening, even if they do. They are usually unaware of the other's feelings, which is why they may think that their partner does not care about them.

The tendency to doubt one's love is extremely common, but dismissive avoidants have it worse than most. They have these conflicting emotions because they need intimate relationships to be happy, and the other person's attention could help them feel more secure in their close relationship. However, due to their high fear of rejection, they are likely to push the other person away. They will often believe that the other person does not love them or that they do not deserve this kind of love and get confused about their feelings for the other person.

6. A strong reaction to the betrayal

Dismissive avoidants often have a very strong reaction to betrayal and may not trust their partners completely, especially if they have been with them for some time. In their minds, it is not worth giving someone a chance if they could easily leave them or hurt them. They are slow to trust, and once they do, the other person will likely be able to sense how cautious they are. If someone hurts them, they will take it much more personally than most people would and may feel like their whole world has been turned upside down.

They will do the following things:

a. Try to forget the betrayal

People who experience betrayal strongly sometimes persuade themselves that what happened wasn't significant or wasn't as bad as it seemed, and they want to move on from what happened rather than wallowing in the betrayal.

If someone hurts them, the dismissive avoidant will try to avoid their feelings about it. They will tell themselves that no one is perfect and that the other person has made a mistake, and they will have to accept this. If the other person tries to discuss it, they might get angry because doing so might make them feel bad about themselves once more.

b. Push away the person who betrayed them

Dismissive avoidants will often push the other person away to stop the hurt. They will tell themselves they are better off without them.

c. Have trouble feeling certain about their relationship

Since their partner betrayed them, the dismissive avoidant person will have trouble feeling certain about their relationship. They will think it is not worth committing to someone who could hurt them again and will think about finding someone else to be with. At the same time, they may feel like their partner does not want them anymore because of what happened, and this could cause them to become angry.

The partner will probably not know how to deal with the dismissive-avoidant's behavior, but they might try to support them in their unhappiness by trying to understand their feelings and help them cope with the situation.

d. Feel much better after avoiding someone

The dismissive avoidant will feel much better after avoiding someone because they can feel in control of what happens and don't have to make themselves vulnerable. They will also want to forget about the betrayal and move on. When the other person tries to talk to them about this, it might make them feel bad again because they don't want to be reminded of how much it hurt. But, if their partner persists in talking to them, they could become angry because they feel like they might be rejected again. Overall, the dismissive avoidant be hesitant to let their partner know how they are feeling.

Dismissive-avoidants in a relationship might have these behaviors regarding their partner, which can make the partner feel sad and insecure. They may not want to be in a relationship because they only see their differences rather than their similarities due to a lack of understanding. Ultimately, these behaviors can lead to conflict in their relationship.

CHAPTER 5

HOW DISMISSIVE AVOIDANTS BREAK UP

L ove, at its best, is a deep and all-consuming feeling. At its worst, it can be fleeting and fickle. It can also be overwhelming and suffocating. So, when a dismissive avoidant breaks up with someone they love, there are a lot of feelings that are involved. The possibility of someone with a dismissive avoidant attachment having a break-up in a relationship is high. The way they handle a break-up is unique.

The following are some of the ways dismissive avoidants deal with a breakup:

1. Pretend they don't feel anything

Dismissive avoidants often have a high opinion of themselves but a low opinion of their partners, which leads them to act as if they have no feelings after a breakup. This might not be a temporary emotional detachment or a lack of care but simply a means of appearing strong and in control. By having an air of "I don't need you or care," the person creates a disconnection that is almost impossible to breach.

This could be seen as the person's way of coping with the debilitating effects of the loss

They will do the following things:

a. Downplay the loss

They will pretend their heart is not broken, or that they did not suffer. By saying things like "I am over you," or, "You were not that great," the person is trying to convince themselves and prove how accepting and non-needy they truly are. This is a way of fooling themselves.

The dismissive avoidant wants to feel that they are not affected by the breakup. This is why they will tell close friends and possibly family members that they are okay and that the break-up was not that bad. By telling others, it helps them to reinforce this idea about themselves.

They do this for two reasons: one, it makes them feel better about themselves; two, it makes the other person think more highly of them. The person may make jokes about the breakup and might even flirt with their ex. While they might not confess their love, they want to let their ex know they are doing fine without them. Doing this makes them feel more confident and less afraid of showing emotions.

Most dismissive avoidants have broken up many times before, so it is only natural for this coping mechanism to surface at one time or another.

b. Trying to play the field

To prove that they are truly not affected by their loss, they will try to find someone else and get into a new relationship immediately. They might become jealous of the partner who has moved on with another person and talk about how bad the relationship was for them and why they should not start dating again.

They will often talk about their ex to justify why they are not happy. They will tell other people that the break-up was not that big of a deal. This way, if someone asks them what happened, all they have to do is say, "Oh, nothing" as an answer. This will help them avoid talking about their feelings and keep up the emotional detachment.

They might even talk about the new person they are seeing and how great things are going between them. They will focus more on the new relationship than anything related to their ex-partner. This way, they can convince themselves and others that they are fine.

c. Trying to forget about the person

In an attempt to forget their ex, they will also tell themselves and others how much better off they are without them. This helps them convince themselves that the breakup was a good thing. Dismissive avoidants tend to be dishonest about themselves and others because of their low self-esteem, so this is no surprise.

They also don't want any reminders of the person or their failed relationship. Only by removing their partner from Facebook, Twitter, or whichever social media platform they use will this be possible. They do this because they want to avoid seeing pictures of them happy with someone else and seeing messages they received from the ex. Jealous feelings can turn into feelings of rejection, so they try their best to ignore these emotions.

By giving up or acting as if they are not attached to the other person, the person is trying to prove they are strong and independent. The person will become emotionally detached and thus unable to have a healthy relationship in the future.

2. Self-harming after a breakup

A common way for a person with dismissive avoidant attachment to deal with grief is to hurt themselves. They have an underlying pain from past wounds and rejections, which makes them lash out in self-hurtful ways. This is especially true for breakups that involve cheating and lying. They will feel mad at themselves for not seeing the warning signs, and they will try to punish themselves by self-harming either physically or emotionally. This is an unconscious attempt to gain control when they feel that it is being taken away from them.

They will do the following things:

a. Physical self-harm

The person will self-harm in one way or another to feel better. The most common form of self-harming behavior is cutting. This relieves their feelings of sadness, guilt, and remorse. It helps them stop hurting for a little while and helps them forget about the bad things that have happened. It also gives them temporary relief so they can sleep better at night.

Self-harming is a way for the person to not think about the pain they are trying to block out. When they are in physical pain, they think about that, not how lost and lonely they feel. They will self-harm to forget about their problems, no matter what state their physical body is in. This behavior can become a habit and is very hard to stop once it has gotten out of control.

b. Starve themselves or binge eat

They will often starve themselves or binge eat when they feel bad. This results from their inability to express their feelings. As a result of eating too much, they will gain weight and lose their physical health. This reinforces their feelings of being worthless because they know they need to care for themselves more but do not know how. They will feel like they are a burden to other people, making them even more unlovable than before. It can also make them feel trapped, scared, and unable to sleep well due to hunger pains in the middle of the night.

The person will often feel embarrassed and ashamed over their lack of self-control, so they will try their best to forget the incident by refusing to talk about it. This makes them withdraw from others and even causes them to blame themselves for all the bad things that have happened because of their poor nutrition and lifestyle.

c. Seek dangerous activities

The person will often seek out dangerous activities in an attempt to feel better about themselves. They will also do things without thinking them through. This can include unsafe sex and reckless driving. These things require physical involvement and makes them forget about their thoughts of being unlovable and worthless. They feel relieved and are able to sleep peacefully as opposed to having nightmares about the past.

The problem is that it usually gets them in trouble and even puts them in jail. In fact, in some cases, death may very well be the consequence. In any case, they will feel bad afterward because they made the wrong choice. Because it only makes things worse, they keep putting themselves in perilous situations in an effort to escape their reality.

d. Self-medicating with alcohol or drugs

Another way they deal with the bad feelings is to use drugs or alcohol in an attempt to numb their emotions. It makes them feel better for a while, and then they will start feeling bad again once the spell wears off.

When they stop using these substances, they might experience physical withdrawal, which involves sleepiness, anxiety, and irritability. They may then return to drugs or alcohol to return to feeling pleasure again. This cycle can continue indefinitely. It also makes them feel ashamed and guilty for putting themselves in harm's way to escape their problems.

Harming behaviors are a way for the dismissive avoidant to deal with the pain they feel inside. It's a way for them to feel something rather than nothing and relieve themselves from their state of mind. It is common for those who have experienced emotional abuse or neglect in their life, and it can become an all-consuming habit that can cause great harm to themselves and others.

3. Seek Revenge

They often feel so undeserving of love that they will become vengeful. They will find ways to avenge themselves against everyone who has ever wronged them because they are not happy with the way their life is turning out. They feel useless and powerless to change their situation, so they seek revenge by doing things that are not socially acceptable, like violence or other crimes.

They believe they have been mistreated in the past, so it is okay for them to mistreat others. The more pain and abuse someone has received, the more damage it does on a mental level.

They will do the following things:

a. Use violence

Dismissive avoidants will often use violence in a passive-aggressive way. They are the sort of individuals that will remain silent when their behavior is criticized. To get back at the person for something that has been bothering them for a very long time, they will often plot behind the scenes. This is a way for them to feel something, even if it is only in their mind.

Dismissive-avoidants are especially prone to violence and other crimes when they feel that they have been disrespected, mistreated, or cast aside. It is their way of coping with their pain and getting back at the person who has caused them so much distress in their life.

The main thing that dismissive avoidant wants to prove is how much worse they can make things for the people who have hurt them. They want to make those people regret ever doing those things to them, whether intentional or not.

b. Spread rumors and gossip

Often, the dismissive avoidant will not say anything directly about their plans for revenge. Instead, they will make others say it for them by spreading rumors and gossip about their ex-lover, ex-friend, and any other people who have hurt them. They will try to get others to help them with their plans for revenge.

Unlike the actively aggressive person, the dismissive avoidant will not say anything up front about what they are doing or anything negative about the person who has caused them harm. Instead, they will smile and pretend it doesn't bother them so they can easily conceal what they are trying to accomplish. In an effort to win back the person's favor, they may even act as though they have already forgiven them. This way, they can easily get their revenge on the person and yet do not have to feel guilty about what they are doing.

The purpose of spreading rumors is to disrupt the lives of those who have caused them harm, whether it be family members, friends, or partners. It causes confusion and chaos, which leads to emotional distress for everyone involved. They might even try to get someone else to do their dirty work for them by misleading them into doing something that will make the person look bad in front of others.

c. Threaten suicide

Another way that they can get their revenge is to threaten suicide. This way, the angry and hurt person who has wronged them will feel guilty, which makes the dismissive avoidant happier. This is their way of feeling something; although it is usually just a threat, it can still cause some damage in the real world and the minds of themselves and others.

Dismissive avoidants often do not express their true emotions and intentions. As a result, it will be very challenging for those close to them to determine whether the person is telling the truth or not.

d. Act crazy to ruin their ex's reputation

They might even act crazy in front of other people to make their ex-lover look bad. They are people who love to stir up trouble.

They may say things like, "Your mother and father are so embarrassed by you. I can't believe what you are doing to yourself." This way, the person who has been mistreated will feel embarrassed and constantly worry that their family is not proud of them anymore. They will take this as a personal insult which makes them feel even worse about themselves, all because of what they are going through with their ex-lover.

The dismissive avoidant is hoping to make the ex-lover feel guilty about the things that they have done to them. They want them to reminisce on those memories and realize their actions were hurtful and wrong. They want them to regret everything they have done to damage the relationship. This way, they can feel better, knowing they finally got revenge on the person who hurt them.

A part of being dismissive avoidant is making the people who have harmed them feel bad about themselves and their actions. They are not direct about this. They are very concerned with how the people around them will view them, especially if they say something directly to the person's face. They want everyone to know they were right, no matter what happened.

4. Mourning

They do not voice any feelings about the fact that they are going through a lot of pain and suffering. They will always be smiling, no matter how bad things may be for them, as they struggle to express their emotions to others.

They will do the following things:

a. Become distant and unresponsive

They will be distant from their friends and family members, especially in times of emotional distress, as they do not want to be a burden. They will also pretend everything is fine.

Dismissive avoidants often seem happy on the outside but are hurting inside. They can maintain a good surface because they do not want to bring anyone else any unnecessary emotional distress. They will constantly put on a brave face and try to act happy even when everything inside is screaming at them. Mourning is one of the more intense and emotional stages of grief that people can go through. But to outsiders, the grieving person will be the same person they have always known.

b. Severe depression and anxiety

They may also be grieving and depressed. They may begin to believe they are incapable of doing anything right. They will also have severe bouts of anxiety. This is the stage where they will lose all hope in their relationships. This stage is usually a result of a major betrayal or some other form of emotional trauma in their life where they have been damaged so badly that they cannot get up off the ground and move on with their lives again. They will feel as if they are being constantly judged and ridiculed by everyone they know.

Other people can easily manipulate them because they do not have much faith in their skills and abilities. They believe they can do nothing to make people see who they are and how much they have accomplished. This is one of the reasons why they are not as confident in themselves as they could be. This can cause them to fall apart because they feel like nothing is working anymore.

The dismissive avoidant will not be able to cope with the anxiety and depression and will begin to act strange and out of character. They will become clingy and needy, so those around them will pay attention to them. Their self-esteem will be at an all-time low.

d. Have nightmares of the ex

Dismissive avoidants may dream of their exes in their sleep. They will then have trouble sleeping because of the fear that they have for their dreams and thoughts.

This is one of the worst parts of a dismissive-avoidant's life because they have already given up so much of themselves to the person who hurt them. They may begin to believe they will never have any fun in their lives again. They may feel like nothing else matters anymore except for dealing with what happened during this relationship. They begin to look at every relationship as if it were a prison sentence.

Mourning is one of the more important stages that a person can go through when it comes to dealing with their emotions. Dismissive avoidants need to learn how to deal with these emotions in order to break from the downward spiral and get on with their lives.

5. Wish for reconciliation

Dismissive avoidant fears are usually at their peak when they realize that the person who left them has moved on and is interested in someone else. This will often make them realize that they have not done anything to make themselves better as a person, and will feel as though they will be stuck in the past forever.

When a dismissive-avoidant comes to this realization, they will begin to wish things could have been different with their exes, often because they still love them deeply and do not want to lose that connection forever. They will begin to question whether or not they are ready for a new relationship or if they should wait until they find someone who truly understands them and loves them. They will be in constant grief and anxiety regarding this topic.

They will do the following things:

a. Reminisce about the past

They will begin to have flashbacks of all the good times they had with their exes because they think about them all the time. They will try to get those images out of their minds sometimes because they know it is not healthy for them, but that does not mean they will be able to stop it from happening. These flashbacks may come back to them no matter where they go and what they are doing and they struggle to cope with it on a daily basis.

b. Call or text the ex

Dismissive avoidants may call or text their exes at any time of the night because they miss them so much and need reassurance that nothing bad will ever happen between them again. They will not get this re-assurance however, and their exes will begin to block their calls. This can make a dismissive avoidant feel as if they are not worth anything at all, making them want to call even more. It is a never-ending cycle.

c. Try to reconnect with the ex

Dismissive avoidants will try to reconnect with their exes in any way they can because they want them back in their lives and feel as if they need them to survive.

If an ex does respond and the relationship is rekindled, the dismissive avoidant will want to spend as much time with them as possible, despite not being completely honest about their feelings. They fear they could lose them again if they express how they feel or if their past behavior continues into this relationship.

d. Promises to change

Dismissive avoidants may promise to change themselves for their exes so they will want them in their lives again. If they feel they need to put on a show for this person, then that is what they will do.

Dismissive avoidance is an attachment style that is considered unhealthy. Still, it can be extremely difficult for the person with this behavior to do anything about it. There is still hope if someone tries hard enough to get over their ex and get on with their lives, even though it could take some time to do so.

These behaviors can be extremely damaging, especially if the dismissive avoidant is not given the proper treatment or support. This behavior can be difficult to work through and can cause much pain and suffering for all involved.

PART 3

OVERCOMING YOUR DISMISSIVE AVOIDANCE

CHAPTER 6

AM I DISMISSIVE AVOIDANT?

The first step toward tackling an issue is to recognize it. Identifying whether you have a dismissive-avoidant attachment will allow you to take the steps needed to start having great relationships. It will also help you understand your relationship dynamics and what is hindering you from success.

Signs that You Are Dismissive Avoidant

1. You don't want to depend on someone, and you don't want them to depend on you.

Dismissive avoidants feel comfortable with this arrangement. They want to take care of themselves and be independent. They find it unnecessary for someone to take care of them and don't want them to do so. Therefore, they will behave in a way that lets them do what they like without worrying about someone else's desires or presence.

If you feel uncomfortable being dependent on someone else, you are likely dismissive avoidant. It doesn't imply that you can't or won't rely on others. It just means that you must be aware of your decisions' consequences to take care of your interests first.

To further explain...

Because of the things you have been exposed to, you have developed beliefs that you should be independent and take care of yourself. These feelings are deeply rooted in your personality. When someone is dependent on you, they tend to make you feel uncomfortable, and therefore you behave in a way that causes them to step back. Dismissive avoidants are not afraid to dependent on someone, especially for the right person or the right reasons. However, when someone is dependent on them (or the situation has been forced upon them), they become victims of their feelings and situations. It is almost as if their personality has a mind of its own, and they cannot control it and are unaware of what it does.

2. You never want to "let down" anyone

Many people will ask for the help of their friends, families, and co-workers at some point in their lives. Many say, "I don't want to burden you," or "I know I need your help, but I don't want to put you out." These types of comments are not meant to be hurtful or a sign of being unappreciative. They are just a way of showing that someone is respectful and considerate of their partners' needs, even though they don't want to burden them. If a person feels the need to say this to someone, it is usually because they think that person has a right to know when they need help.

If you tend to say things like "I don't want to put you out" or "I know I need your help, but I don't want to burden you," you are probably dismissive avoidant.

To further explain...

You do not want to "let down" someone because you don't want to feel as though you are dependent on them. Not only that, but it is not good for your self-image and self-esteem. "Because I am a self-sufficient individual, I do not require the assistance of others. I must rely on myself." This way, you will achieve the independence you have always desired.

In your eyes, you are respectful and considerate of the people around you by ensuring you do not depend on them. This is what happens when you are a dismissive avoidant. You tend to distort the things around you and give them a different meaning. You do this because you believe it is right and better for you in the long run. Therefore, you are reluctant to ask for help, even if it is just a small matter.

3. You don't like to be close to people.

Dismissive avoidants are not interested in making themselves too vulnerable to others or letting them into their life because they do not to risk of getting hurt by letting others see who they are. Most will deny that they are afraid of being close to others and claim that they don't mind getting close to people. However, the truth is that they have a different ways of showing their closeness. Most just smile and pretend they are happy when they're not or act like they care when they don't.

If you are someone with a dismissive-avoidant attachment, you will likely be unable to get close to someone easily. You will keep your distance until you feel comfortable enough to let them in. Then, perhaps you will get too close, and this will cause you to lose your confidence and feel unsafe.

To further explain...

When you get too close with someone, the person might see parts of your life or personality that you did not want them to see. This will trigger your insecurities and make you defensive and resistant. As a result, you become negative and doubt yourself, which leads to your attitude of not wanting to get close to others. This is just a defense mechanism that you have developed because you are afraid to let others in and share your life with them.

Dismissive avoidants are very selective in choosing their friends. They will not simply jump into a new relationship or environment due to what they have been through. Given their trust issues, it will take time for them to open up and let people in so they can start bonding with them. When someone becomes too close, it will often lead them to feel unsafe.

4. You easily get stressed out

Dismissive avoidants are often afraid that others will judge them and make them feel bad about themselves. This can lead to high levels of stress.

When your stress levels go up, you might start to do things that make you look anxious. For example, you might walk around looking tense or look at the clock often. You might also continuously check your phone and ensure you have no unread messages or notifications. You might find yourself trying to avoid people and doing things independently to protect yourself from getting close to others.

To further explain…

Dismissive avoidant are very sensitive to the moods of others. They do not just become stressed whenever someone around them has a bad day. They are afraid that their actions will cause these people's moods to change for the worse, which is one of the reasons they avoid close contact. They might pretend they are not anxious while being very anxious and frightened that others will see through their façade and start judging them or have harsh feelings towards them. Their whole life has been based on hiding who they are and what they feel, so to see someone else show these parts of themselves is terrifying and causes them to lose their composure.

5. You fear being alone.

Dismissive avoidants are unable to find happiness in being alone. They are reluctant to be alone with their thoughts and feelings because of the significant amount of suffering and rejection they have experienced in the past. Although some people might criticize you for being too independent or not social enough, in truth, you prefer being with other people.

Dismissive avoidants have high sensitivity, which means that even when they are alone, their mind is very active. This makes them anxious and fearful of being on their own.

To further explain...

Many people become dismissive avoidant because they have been hurt or abandoned by their family, partner, or friends. It is likely that they have learned to be distrustful of people. They may also have experienced being picked on or rejected by others and have developed a negative outlook on life. When someone criticizes them, it triggers this negativity, making them believe that everyone is out to make their lives difficult.

6. You might be an "entitled" person

You may act like an entitled person if you have a dismissive-avoidant attachment style. Specifically, it will be about your rights and expectations for things such as attention, validation, or approval. If someone does not give you these things that you feel entitled to, then they will upset you or threaten your sense of happiness.

While this sounds like something you would expect from a "narcissistic" person, it is not the same. Narcissists think they are entitled to things but lack empathy and feel no remorse for what they do, which causes them to be entitled. Narcissists might think they deserve special consideration and attention, but they don't become upset when they don't get their way or receive all of the attention from others. But in the case of dismissive avoidants, if someone does not give them what they want, it can make them feel hurt or rejected.

To further explain...

Someone with a dismissive-avoidant attachment style is not likely to be insecure about their looks or talents. Instead, they are worried that others will judge them for who they are and what they feel. They are more concerned with being taken advantage of or having others control them.

Therefore, when someone else does not take care of their needs or demands, it makes them feel angry and upset because they think this means that the other person thinks they are insignificant. However, you may later find out that this was just something your mind created due to your negative outlook on emotional intimacy. Because of this, you are more inclined to feel disappointed in people than angry with them.

7. You might be a "Mr./Mrs. Fix-It."

Another characteristic of a dismissive-avoidant is their trait of being a "Mr./Mrs. Fix-It." When someone acts differently from what they expect, they will try to fix them to prevent someone from getting hurt or angry. They may also try to "make" other people do what they want.

This trait is not necessarily bad. It can be beneficial if you want to take care of your friends and family, but only if those people are willing to let you take care of them. If not, you can turn into a "Mr./Mrs. Fix-It" at every turn, making you feel frustrated and upset because you take care of everyone else, and they do not appreciate it.

To further explain...

Dismissive-avoidants may also take on the role of being a "mother" or "father" type of person. They want to make sure everyone else is safe and happy, but this can make other people feel hurt because they are not being treated like an equal.

8. You might have a "situational" personality

A situational personality is not rigid or consistent. It is unpredictable and does not have an overall "tone" or "mood." You can have a different outlook on life depending on the time of day, who you are with, and what is going on in your life.

Although this can be true of almost everyone to some degree, those with a dismissive-avoidant attachment style are more likely to do this because they do not feel connected enough to anyone or anything else. This can cause their personality and behavior to change randomly without warning.

To further explain...

Dismissive avoidants will typically look out for themselves first, and if they do not get what they want, they might become frustrated and angry. They may also be quick to anger instead of taking responsibility for their behavior.

To avoid being hurt or rejected by others, they will change how they act or will expect things from others based solely on their mood. This can make them appear difficult to understand because it will cause them to behave in inconsistent and unpredictable ways. They may seem out of sorts or even "crazy."

10. You may be fixated on a certain topic

Dismissive avoidants are constantly thinking about the past and future. They are either thinking about things from a negative point of view or fixating on things that are unrealistic and unlikely to happen.

This is because they feel anxious when faced with a problem. As a result, they frequently fail to notice the good things going on around them and lose out on all the beautiful things that happen every day.

You may be stuck in the past a lot, which can make you feel "trapped" and unable to move on. If you want to move forward with your life, you must let go of the past, but this is easier said than done.

To further explain...

As opposed to being grateful for what they already have and all the good things that have occurred, dismissive avoidants often focus on what they "don't have" or "what they missed out on." They frequently dwell on the "what ifs" and "what might have been."

Instead of watching for the positive, they will also be fixated on the negative and obsess about it until it consumes their lives. They may also stress themselves out trying to control everything around them because they are always thinking about how things might go wrong.

This can cause them to become "stuck," making it almost impossible for any progress to be made.

11. You think it is okay to lie and deceive others.

Dismissive avoidants will often try to avoid feelings of shame, guilt, and fear by convincing themselves it is okay to behave in whatever way they can, even if it means lying or deceiving others. They may explain this behavior by claiming that lying and deception are "essential" and "the best approach" to accomplish their goals. This causes them not to value honesty or trustworthiness in another person. They may lie without feeling guilty, making others feel misunderstood or betrayed.

To further explain...

Dismissive avoidants often tell themselves they are "not a bad person" and do not have to feel afraid, ashamed, or guilty. This can cause them to think it is okay to lie, deceive or cheat others. They have trouble feeling remorseful, which makes it difficult for them to admit their wrongdoings for the sake of being forgiven by others. They want to see themselves as better than the rest, so they might feel it is okay to manipulate others by controlling how they think or perceive something.

12. You might not worry about the consequences of your actions.

A dismissive avoidant will often not feel guilty or fearful about what they do because they feel like they have a right to do so. Because of this, they are less likely to think about their actions' consequences on others or themselves. They likely feel it is okay to control other people's thoughts and feelings in this way.

You may not be worried about the outcome of your actions either. Instead, you might feel that you are always "right" or that you have no reason to worry. You may also think that people will not find out about what you are doing anyway.

To further explain...

Dismissive avoidants will often not feel guilty about what they do because they feel it is "okay" to do whatever they want. This can make them do morally wrong things without thinking about the consequences. They may also feel like they cannot be controlled or manipulated by others, even if they are dishonest with them.

Dismissive-avoidants tend to think they can manipulate others and control their feelings, thoughts, and actions. They believe that everyone else has done bad things in the past, so it is okay for them to do the same thing. They may also have trouble feeling remorseful about their actions, making it hard for someone else to forgive them.

13. You are secretive.

Dismissive avoidants tend to be secretive about their own lives, but not necessarily for any bad reason. They may feel like other people do not care about them or what is going on in their lives, and this causes them to keep secrets. This is so that no one else can reject or hurt them by knowing too much about them.

You may also try hiding your feelings or thoughts because you believe they are "wrong" or not welcome. This can cause you to keep to yourself even when talking with people, which might make them feel uncomfortable.

To further explain...

Being secretive is often caused by a lack of trust between people. People who lack trust tend to be paranoid and suspicious of others, which makes them hide things.

Dismissive avoidants tend to think that what they do is not important enough to tell other people. They might feel like other people will not care about their problems, so they keep things to themselves. This can make them feel detached from other people. They also believe that others will reject or abandon them if they get to know them too much. They might also feel that others will not understand what they are going through, which causes them to keep their feelings and thoughts hidden from others.

Being secretive is sometimes caused by childhood abuse, where a child is told to keep secrets from their family members out of fear of being abused again. They may feel like they cannot share their thoughts and feelings with others because they might get rejected by them or mocked if they do. They might also feel like what they are going through is not important enough to talk about, making it hard for them to share their feelings with someone else.

14. You might want to be "cooler" than others.

Dismissive avoidants tend to compare themselves to others, which can cause them to feel like they do not measure up. Because of this, you will likely try your best to be better than others.

You may be very careful about how you dress, talk, how much money you spend, or anything that can make others think of you as "cooler" than them. You may try to buy things that are more expensive than others, dress in a style that is not as common, or read books that impress others. This can cause you to be likable and impressive to others, but it can also make it more challenging for you to get close to them.

To further explain...

Dismissive avoidants tend to feel less confident about themselves, which can cause them to compare themselves with others. They may feel inadequate when they compare themselves to others, so they strive to appear "better" or "cooler" in whatever they do.

Dismissive avoidants might also feel like they need to impress other people. They may measure their success by how many compliments or praise they get. They may feel like this is the only way to get someone else's attention.

15. You are not open to change

Dismissive avoidants tend to be resistant to change. They may believe that anything new is a waste of their time and that the old methods were superior. People who do not want to change will often refuse new ideas or to venture into things they are afraid of trying.

To further explain...

Dismissive avoidants tend to believe that what is new is not special or interesting because it is different than what they are used to. Because of this, they may have difficulty adapting to change. They feel like they have more control when things stay the same. They also tend to be guarded with their feelings so they won't get hurt again. This makes it hard for them to get close to other people and adapt to the changes in their life, such as moving to a new home or changing schools.

Keep in mind that these indications are not definitive. Exhibiting some of these traits does not mean that you are necessarily a dismissive avoidant, but they could be signs that you are. It is also important to consult a psychologist or counselor to determine if your behaviors match these indicators. Knowing these indications can also help you deal with this character trait so you do not cause yourself harm.

CHAPTER 7

UNDERSTANDING MY TRIGGERS

Understanding what triggers particular emotions can help us regulate our responses. By regulating our emotions, we can gradually develop a more stable attachment style and control our responses to events and feelings inside a relationship. Understanding what triggers emotions can help you develop better relationships simply by learning to regulate your reactions and responses to your specific triggers.

Common Triggers

1. Criticism

Criticism can trigger our deepest insecurities about ourselves and our values. It is a form of communication that we interpret as both dismissive and critical of us. With a dismissive-avoidant attachment style, it can be hard to differentiate criticism from constructive feedback—and, therefore, hard to know how to respond. This attachment style can make it challenging for us to receive criticism with an open heart and mind, even when it is constructive.

Dismissive avoidants can have difficulties constructively receiving feedback because it can the feeling of being can cause them to respond the same way they did as children. Criticism can trigger a critical part within the mind of the dismissive-avoidant, which tells them they are not good enough, that they don't deserve anything more, and that their value is only as useful as their usefulness to others. Thus, the person is motivated to satisfy others very passively. They may even feel that they deserve to be treated badly because they don't deserve anything more than that.

In many cases, criticism can lead to a lot of emotional turmoil and distress within the dismissive avoidant, driving them to act out in excessive ways such as:

a. Taking refuge in self-absorption

Criticism is a complex issue and can be carried out in many ways. It can manifest itself as an over-abundance of criticism of the self, or an over-abundance of criticism of others. However, within a dismissive-avoidant attachment style, criticism will often be aimed at the self rather than others. Many people have experienced criticism that they felt was unjustified in one way or another and thus have responded by taking refuge in self-absorption. Because of their hypersensitivity to rejection, they are motivated to withdraw into themselves so that they won't become any more vulnerable than they already are.

Regarding a dismissive avoidant, the criticism they were once power-less against can be difficult for them to process. Because this type of criticism is not received in the proper context of a healthy relationship, it can damage their trust in the people trying to communicate with them.

b. Showing moodiness and emotional withdrawal

Emotional withdrawal can be a way for the dismissive avoidant to reduce their emotional vulnerability to others. They may emotionally withdraw after receiving criticism, hoping to avoid additional con-flict and, thus, further criticism. The dismissive avoidant will seek to protect themselves in this manner, but others may see such actions as offensive. This can cause the dismissive avoidant to appear emotionally withdrawn and unresponsive.

When dealing with criticism that the dismissive avoidant does not understand or feel is appropriate for them, they may refuse to talk about it because of their hypersensitivity around rejection and their desire to avoid vulnerability. In this case, the dismissive avoidant may first claim that they are not feeling well and thus avoid the conver-sation. However, when it does become necessary for the dismissive avoidant to address their problem and discuss it with you, they may find themselves acting in a manner that resembles emotional with-drawal or moodiness.

c. Becoming overtalkative

Dismissive avoidants can be overtalkative when they need to com-municate something important in order to maintain a sense of control within a relationship. Those with this attachment style can have difficulties listening and accepting what others say because of their hypersensitivity to rejection and hurt feelings. Thus, the only way that the dismissive avoidant can keep control is through actually talking a lot. They may talk so much that others may find their behavior offensive and annoying. The intent of the person with this attachment style is not necessarily to make others feel uncomfortable or bad, it is their way of communicating what is important to them and trying to maintain control.

d. Using other people's problems as a way to deal with emotional unhappiness

Dismissive avoidants may find themselves becoming overly involved in what others are going through in an effort to avoid experiencing their own painful emotions. They may also use other people to deal with and distract them from the negative feelings that they experience in a relationship.

e. Being overly needy, demanding, or controlling towards their partner

The dismissive avoidant may become overly aggressive during arguments and make demands on others (to the point of being controlling) in an attempt to feel confident. They may also become needy and demanding to keep others close, sometimes resorting to threats and manipulation to get others to do things for them.

Criticism is difficult for a dismissive avoidant to handle since it is such a sensitive issue. This trigger can make the person feel that their true emotions and inner motives are being judged negatively, thus triggering a lot of shame. A person with this style is usually afraid to express their opinions in any argument as they may believe that they are wrong, and they don't want to be judged, so they will choose to be passive and hold back on saying what they feel should be said, even if it is important to them.

2. Expectations

Expectations are another common trigger for dismissive avoidants, particularly when these expectations are unrealistic.

Expectations can cause a great deal of emotional upheaval and distress in the dismissive avoidant, causing them to behave in extreme ways, such as:

a. Becoming overly controlling

Unmet expectations lead to feelings of insecurity in the dismissive avoidant, and they are more likely to react using controlling behavior to make themselves feel better. This can cause them to become very demanding . They may have unrealistic expectations that others should fulfill their needs for them, and they frequently exhibit excessive levels of control over others, to the point where they feel entitled to have their demands met.

This behavior is almost always a reaction to the hurt and pain that the person is feeling rather than an attempt to hurt or control others. In these circumstances, particularly when the dismissive-avoidant is unable to live up to their own standards, they frequently feel that no one will be able to meet their requirements, leading them to become extremely demanding of other people's behavior. This requires other people to be there for them in ways that are not possible or realistic.

b. Becoming despondent and morose

If the need for control is not met, then the dismissive avoidant might turn to feeling sorry for themselves, becoming despondent and morose. This can become a coping mechanism so they don't have to acknowledge their feelings of hurt and work through them in a healthy way (such as communicating with their loved ones or working on a solution). Instead, they regress into acting like children who were abandoned by someone who should have been taking care of them. In some instances, a person may regress into an acting-out behavior and become angry, aggressive, and demanding towards others.

Becoming despondent and morose indicates that the person is too ashamed and sensitive to handle criticism. They may feel completely hopeless or worthless, unable to solve their problems or understand why things are going wrong in their lives, thus making their feelings of disappointment, pain, and fear so much worse.

c. Becoming clingy and overly needy for reassurance

If a person doesn't feel they are getting what they need from their loved one, they will become clingy and demanding to make sure that the others can meet their needs. This is a common reaction when a person feels insecure. Often these demands are seen as inconsiderate or self-centered: they don't care what they are doing to the other person. In extreme cases, the dismissive avoidant may believe that their loved one should be able to read their mind and know what they need, becoming very demanding and angry if their needs are not met. Instead of dealing with the real problem (their own feelings of insecurity), the dismissive avoidant expects others to meet their needs, which is unrealistic and unfair to both parties.

This behavior, again, is caused by the person's mother or primary caregiver leaving them as a child. It shows that the dismissive avoidant does not feel their needs can be met by anyone else but their loved one. It is a sign of insecurity and abandonment, brought on by feeling helpless and powerless when they were a child and needed someone to take care of them.

d. Becoming disinterested, detached, and cold

If their need for control is not met, the dismissive avoidant might become distant and cold toward the other person. They will become emotionally unavailable to their loved one, becoming non-communicative and detached. Due to the individual's insecurity about their own sentiments and their loved one's feelings toward them, this can strain relationships.

This behavior is also a sign of guilt and shame. The person feels like they are not good enough and deserve to be abandoned. This behavior can come about after a traumatic event, such as abuse or neglect, where their needs were not met by the people who should have been doing so, or where their feelings were ignored or shamed by the caregiver so often that it made them certain that no one could meet those needs for them.

The best way to deal with these issues is to communicate them to your loved ones and discuss ways you would like things to improve or be handled differently. For example, if you feel your loved one isn't meeting your needs and treats you poorly, tell them how you feel. Let them know this is not okay with you and make it clear that it bothers you.

3. Pressure

Due to childhood wounds, pressure to open up or be more vulnerable is one of the major triggers for a dismissive-avoidant individual. It is a large part of their self-defense mechanism, as they need to feel as though they are strong and can deal with any pressure that comes their way.

When the pressure gets them, they will react through different methods, including:

a. Fleeing, or a desire to flee

One of the most frequent responses demonstrates their discomfort with emotional demands or vulnerability. Being asked how they feel when they don't want to express their feelings tends to make them feel that others are trying to "get into their head" and control them, which they do not like. They tend to react by putting emotional walls, so there is no longer a connection. They may leave the room, leave the house, break up with their partner or turn cold toward them in response to this pressure rather than dealing with their own negative emotions and allowing themselves to open up and get hurt again.

b. Resisting or denying the feeling

Some people learn how to repress their emotions and will do so whenever they feel overwhelmed by them. They will build walls between themselves and their loved ones in order to prevent feeling as though they are being attacked by the emotions that arise, or as though someone is attempting to get inside of their heads. They may become angry or upset because they feel their partner is "controlling" them. This is usually the coping mechanism they use when they feel as though they are being pressured to open up and express their feelings. They will want to be in control of that part of their life and will react defensively rather than sharing themselves with their loved ones freely.

c. Engaging in smear campaigns or power struggles

This is where one person tries to manipulate others into doing something they don't want to do. They will often make a scene to communicate their disapproval of something their loved one has said, done, or something that was not previously discussed. They may also create a new topic and build it up for days, weeks, months, or even years until it becomes a heated argument. This happens because some people get enjoyment from the misery of another person's life as well as holding on to unresolved issues.

They do this to avoid talking about their true feelings, and because it gives them a sense of control in the relationship. It makes them feel as though they are better than the other person, but they are really making the relationship more difficult by getting their own way.

Pressure is a very effective way to make a dismissive avoidant person feel as though they are being controlled, making them feel like they need to take a defensive stance. The more defensive they become, the fewer problems they are willing to discuss. This makes it harder for them to resolve issues and maintain a relationship because they refuse to share their true feelings.

A dismissive avoidant person believes they will not be loved if they open up to their partner and express their feelings. The problem with this is that when you don't open up, you miss out on the opportunity to see how much your partner loves and cares about you. You are also missing out on opportunities to communicate with them in ways other than through anger or hurtfulness.

Knowing what triggers your defensive response is the first step to having a good relationship. Once you have identified the problem, you will then be able to treat it and will have more chance of building strong and healthy relationships.

CHAPTER 8

MANAGING MY EMOTIONS

E motions are a part of every moment. You can't choose to "feel nothing" or numb yourself from hurt, disappointment, or anger. It's normal to have emotions, and you would never want to hide them. However, some people tend to dismiss, ignore or make light of their feelings as they differ greatly from their objective reality. Problems arise when you do not trust your feelings and react openly to intense emotions or experiences.

When our emotional conflicts or pain are too overwhelming to acknowledge, we tend to disconnect from them. Until we feel safe enough to acknowledge our strongest emotions, they will continue to lurk deep inside us. Disconnecting from your feelings is a coping mechanism that allows you to protect yourself from getting hurt, rejected, or criticized by others but it comes at the expense of pushing people away.

Knowing how to manage your emotions is important when to comes to changing your life and developing a more balanced and healthy self-image. When you learn how to react to various circumstances, you might also feel some relief from your emotional pain.

Self-Regulation Techniques

The following techniques can be used to connect with your emotions healthily and help you to manage them:

1. Communicate your feelings

Communication is a great way to manage our emotions because it allows us to experience and try new ways of dealing with problems. Communication also helps to develop a bond of trust with another person. This is one of the most effective ways to manage your emotions.

The following are ways in which you can communicate your feelings:

a. By being assertive and specific

Instead of assuming that the other person understands what you want or need them to do, explain how you feel and what you need.

For example:

- *"I am feeling uncomfortable when you __________ (things that make you feel uncomfortable). Could we please change the way we do it? Let's try __________ instead."*

- *"I feel hurt when you __________ (actions that hurt you). Can you try to do things differently?"*

- *"You make me feel __________ whenever you __________ (actions or words that affect your emo-*

tions). I am willing to try and do something different."

It's important to avoid saying: "Stop doing that." This kind of statement is too vague, and it doesn't allow the other person the space to work with you. If they can't understand what they are doing wrong, they will not be able to change.

Always keep your door open for discussion, and state what is bothering you clearly and gently. When you ask someone for help or assistance, it's also crucial to be polite and non-demanding. You may want to state what you feel like doing instead of forcing someone to do things your way.

b. Show you are calm and open-minded.

Being a dismissive-avoidant person can make you feel like you are under attack when you are not alone. So it is important to express your feelings, not in a harsh way but in a calm and friendly manner, to show your true intentions. This will enable others to understand what's happening inside you.

For example:

- *"I am feeling uncomfortable now because I had misunderstood something that you said _____________ (emotional conflict). Can we talk about it together? I want to change how I react, so it doesn't hurt me."*

- *"I am feeling uncomfortable because you _____________. I want us to have a chat now and try to change the way we do things together. You must*

- *understand what I am going through."*

- *"I feel hurt when you ________________ (emotional conflict). Can we talk about this? I think it would help me if you could help me understand why you did it."*

- *"You make me feel ________________ whenever you ________ (emotional conflict). I feel that I've been treated unfairly. Can we talk about this so that we can solve this issue?"*

It's important not to sound demanding, threatening, or critical. No one wants to feel blamed or attacked because they are guilty of your emotional pain. So it's a good idea to make things clear and to be reasonable instead of angry.

2. Soothe your emotions

This is another way of managing your emotions and preventing them from getting out of control. When you are sad or irritated, there are easy things you may do to help yourself feel better.

a. Exercise

Exercise helps you clear your head and distract your mind, which will help you relax. In addition to releasing endorphins that lower stress, physical activity is a great method for controlling your emotions and getting respite from your troubles. This is an effective method for decreasing stress and alleviating tension so you can see life more clearly.

The following are some basic exercises you can use to help you relax:

1. Walking Outside

This is a great way to remove yourself from the stressful stimulus and walk your problems off. The fresh air will help you figure out what you need, and it helps to stimulate the thinking process. This is also a good idea if you feel irritable towards others because getting outside will take your mind off it and let you unwind.

It is recommended that you walk for 20 minutes a day. Walking outside is very beneficial for your mental health, but you can still exercise at home if you're stuck indoors, or it's too chilly outside. You can walk around the rooms and do small exercises that don't require a lot of energy.

Exercising your body to stimulate and relieve your mind can help calm you and think clearer. In this way, your emotions will become less of a problem.

2. Jogging or running

Like walking outside, jogging or running helps clear your head from negative thoughts and stressors; it also helps burn away unwanted tension. The release of energy from the body is a good way of releasing tension from your mind, so the more you can jog or run, the better. This is especially helpful if you are running through new places.

It is recommended that you run or jog for 30 minutes a day. You can go for jogs in the morning or before bed at night. This is a healthy way to exercise your body and mind to better manage your emotions.

3. Dancing

Dancing is a terrific way to express oneself because it is similar to singing or acting out your thoughts and emotions. It's a good way to let go of stress and become more flexible and expressive, which will help you manage your emotions better.

Dancing helps you release your emotions and relieve tension, so you will feel better after doing it. It's a great way of venting emotionally and working out how you feel, and it makes you feel more open to change. You can attend a class, or dance in front of a mirror or to your own music. One good thing about dancing is that you have complete freedom to express yourself however you desire. And even if no one else sees or hears you, the freedom of expression will help you feel better because it's just you and your emotions.

4. Exercise Videos

If you can't get outside, exercise videos are also a good alternative that can provide a much-needed release from stress and tension. If you have other duties to perform, such as taking care of children or pets, these videos are quick and convenient ways of getting in your workout without skipping out on personal or family time.

You can learn different routines and perform them in your home; you can also perform them with other people struggling to manage their emotions. This is a healthy way of relieving stress, so it's a good option if you want to manage your emotions and make yourself feel better.

Plenty of exercise videos can help you get fit and relieve tension; some are martial arts themed while others focus on aerobics and simple workouts. They are available online, and in stores, so you have multiple options when searching for one that meets your requirements. Remember not to strain yourself while doing these exercises; if they feel too difficult, it's best to stop.

5. Gardening

Gardening is another way to manage your emotions. It helps you clear your head of stress, and anxiety and do simple tasks without being overwhelmed. It can be done on a daily basis, and it's not something that will require a lot of time.

Gardening also stimulates your mind and helps with creative solutions. It is a great way of managing your emotions because you will be able to solve problems and deal with your feelings in a more healthy way.

You can always start a garden or buy one already formed. Watering, weeding, and taking care of it will help you be more caring towards yourself and others, so your relationships with people will also improve. It's also a great way of getting outside.

Exercise is a great way for people to feel better and manage their emotions. These are only a few options, so feel free to choose the most appropriate one for you. It is essential to continue exercising because it helps your body release tension and stress, thereby enhancing your flexibility, strength, and vitality.

Additionally, it's crucial to make sure that whatever exercise routine you choose to follow is not overly demanding or challenging; it should be something you can perform in the comfort of your own home without feeling overly stressed or under strain.

b. Breathing Techniques

This is a fantastic way to self-soothe and regain emotional control. If you master the art of breathing, you will be able to better control your emotions.

Some breathing techniques include:

a. Abdominal Breathing

It is very important that you breathe evenly and deeply and that your breaths come from your stomach instead of your chest. You will find breathing easier like this when you rest your hands over your stomach area.

This exercise prevents emotional problems and calms you down. It can be very useful in helping you feel relaxed and get some relief from the pain you are experiencing.

How to do it:

Step 1: Put one hand on your abdomen and the other on your chest.

Keep in mind that the hand on your stomach should rise higher than the other hand when you breathe in.

Step 2: Inhale and allow the hand on your chest to sink lower as you breathe in.

Let the other hand rest on top of your stomach, where you should feel a gentle rise as you breathe in deeply.

Step 3: Exhale.

Breathe out fully and slowly. Remember to exhale more slowly than you inhale; this will make you feel very relaxed.

Step 4: Repeat this exercise for 10 minutes, three times a day.

It's crucial that you concentrate on how your body feels during this breathing exercise. It might feel uncomfortable initially, but it will become easier over time.

b. The Positive Thinking Breathing Technique

If you have deep emotional thoughts or experiences, this technique can help you calm down and feel more relaxed. You can also use it when your emotions get out of control. Remember that while doing this exercise, pay attention to how your mind is functioning and how it is reacting to the situation you are in.

This is a very simple but effective way of calming yourself down.

How to do it:

Step 1: Find a peaceful place where you won't be disturbed.

You can sit in a chair facing a wall or sit on a chair in a park without any other people nearby. Anywhere works, as long as it is quiet, calm, and peaceful.

Step 2: Begin by sitting quietly for a few minutes.

Close your eyes, take a few deep breaths, and try to relax. Remember, your goal is to feel calmer and more at peace. So, don't be too hard on yourself if you can't do it right away.

Step 3: As you breathe in, think about the things around you that are causing your feelings or making you upset.

Say them out loud and describe them as much as you can.

For example, if you're feeling upset because of an argument with your friend, say, "I'm feeling upset because my friend yelled at me," or, "I'm feeling upset because my friend didn't help me as I needed."

Step 4: As you breathe and begin to relax, think about the positive experiences around you.

These are the things that have brought you joy and happiness. For example, "I'm happy because I found a new friend," or, "I'm happy because my sister is always there when I need her."

Step 5: Repeat this for 10 minutes three times a day.

This will help you to release your bad emotions and feel more at peace with yourself.

This technique emphasizes awareness of your thoughts, feelings, and sensations so you can discover a better way to deal with them. To do this calming technique properly, you must practice it for about 2 or 3 months. It is essential to comprehend the proper application of this technique, as failure to do so will render it ineffective.

c. Counting Breaths

This technique regulates breathing to achieve a relaxed and peaceful state of mind. It is used to lower your pulse and heart rate, alleviate anxiety, and help you relax.

How to do it:

Step 1: Find a quiet spot and take a seat there.

Make sure your back is straight; this will help keep you focused throughout the exercise.

Step 2: Focus on your breathing and try to empty your mind.

It might not feel easy at first because we are so used to our thoughts, but with practice, you can control your mind. Focus on your breathing. This will assist you in releasing all of the negative emotions that are currently affecting you.

Step 3: Inhale for four counts and exhale for four counts.

Keep your breaths as long as possible, but don't strain yourself.

If you want to calm your mind and relax, keep up the counting. Don't worry about the length of your breaths; focus on the counting and nothing else.

Step 4: Practice this technique for 10–15 minutes a day.

The longer you do this, the better your results will be.

This is one of the simplest techniques that you can do, but it is also very helpful in relieving stress, anxiety, sadness, and anger.

d. The 4-7-8 Breathing Technique

This breathing technique is a variation of the previous one that was mentioned. This breathing exercise was developed by Dr. Andrew Weil, a physician who has spent his whole life researching how to help people maintain good health and treat their illnesses. This technique is very helpful in getting rid of all the negative emotions that are causing you pain or sadness.

The breathing technique makes breathing long, slow, and deep. It also helps in reducing anxiety, mild depression, and anger.

How to do it:

Step 1: Place your tongue behind your teeth and make sure it stays there throughout the exercise.

Step 2: Exhale through your mouth and make a whoosh sound.

Your jaw should be closed but relaxed, so air passes through it easily. Let the air out for about 4 seconds, then inhale for 7 seconds.

Step 3: Hold your breath for 8 seconds and then exhale through your mouth for 4 seconds. Repeat this cycle 8 times or as often as you like.

This technique is used to reduce and relieve stress, anxiety, depression, and anger. It is a very simple technique that helps you to let go of your bad feelings. It should be practiced every day for at least 2 weeks in order for you to start noticing a difference. Your body will change gradually, so it's important to be patient and persevere even if you don't see any changes right away. This technique aims to develop your ability to concentrate and focus better in order to control your thoughts and emotions. If you do not have a goal or something to focus on while performing the exercises, they will not be as effective.

Breathing is a very important factor in everyday life. It is a method of synchronization between our mind and body that helps us be in tune with our environment. Controlling your emotions through breathing is one of the many ways that you can deal with all the stress and anxiety in life. Breathing exercises have a great variety of applications in all areas of your life, so you should use them to maintain health and fitness and improve your quality of life.

3. Challenge your inner critic

The way someone with a dismissive-avoidant attachment style thinks—their inner critic—increases their mistrust of others and the fear that their loved ones will reject or judge them for expressing emotions. Your inner critic is your internal observer who sits outside your awareness and judges every situation by observing it through your eyes alone. One way to cope with the inner critic is to challenge it.

Some ways to challenge the inner critic include:

a. Stop thinking negatively

Your inner critic frequently has something negative to say about what you are doing or how you are being treated when you sit and converse while focusing on it. Instead of listening to the negativity and agreeing with it, say to your inner critic, "No, I disagree." Then ask yourself: "What am I doing that's good?" and start saying positive things.

This is a trick to get your inner critic out of the way long enough to allow you to think constructively. It works because when your inner critic hears you disagree with it, it won't have anything to think about anymore. If you get criticism from others, ask them to tell you why they think that way and then answer your question by starting with, "Surely they must be wrong."

When your inner critic criticizes something harmful, imagine the criticism coming from a stranger and say to yourself, "I accept the fact that people I don't know may have negative opinions about X."

b. Take a constructive approach

When you start to lose control of your emotions, think about the consequences of exploding on the people around you. This will make you feel better and act more constructively. Keep yourself focused on the one thing that is making you angry, no matter how small the problem may seem to others, and bring your focus back onto this one thing whenever it starts to stray from it.

c. Write a letter to your inner critic

Writing out what you would say to your inner critic will help you think more clearly and allow you to speak directly with them. This can be a good way to break through negative thoughts and free yourself of the inner critic's influence.

Inside the letter, determine what you think and feel about the issue, and write what you would say to your inner critic. By confronting your inner critic, you can improve how you feel about yourself.

d. Affirm yourself

When you are sad or upset, you can reverse this trend by filling your mind with positive thoughts and repeating affirmations. Affirmations can be good for getting rid of negative thoughts and replacing them with positive ones. A positive thought can turn into a positive mood, in the same way a negative thought can turn into a negative mood.

What you focus on most becomes what is seen in your mind's eye. You will see what you focus on most; everything else will be minimized or nonexistent. If you repeat affirmations consistently, they will change the way your mind works.

Some good affirmations to recite are:

"I know I can do this."

"I know there are reasons for my feelings."

"I know others care about me."

"I know I can solve my problems."

"I know I am doing my best."

"I have faith in myself."

"I know I am doing good in my life."

"I know there are reasons why I am feeling this way."

"I can feel better."

"The way I feel is okay."

"I care about myself."

"My life is worth living, and people care about me."

Some people find it helpful to repeat affirmations until they start believing them. This can be a good way to improve your self-esteem and feel better about yourself.

Affirmations can take time to work, but if you continue with them, you will eventually believe what the affirmation is telling you about yourself. In the beginning, you may have to say affirmations that do not feel completely true for you. Don't expect too much immediately and keep repeating them until they become part of how you think.

e. Think positively.

You will feel worse when your inner critic makes you think negatively about yourself or your circumstances. You can stop or reduce these feelings by thinking positively about the situation. The more you think positively, the better you will feel. If you start to feel worse, change your thoughts about the situation, and your inner critic will stop making you feel bad.

How to do it:

To start practicing positive thinking:

- Bring a positive thought into your head at any random time during the day (not when negative thoughts come up).

- Focus on that thought for 30 seconds and then drop it from your mind.

- Keep repeating this until you can do it without even thinking about it.

- Start thinking positively about neutral things, like a sunset or a fluffy cloud.

- Practice holding the positive thoughts in your head for longer and longer until you can hold the positive thoughts for the full 30 seconds without letting any negative thoughts enter your mind.

- Once you can do this, practice these techniques when something is making you feel bad in order to change how you feel about it.

As an alternative method, put all your focus into one part of your body (like your hand) and allow yourself to feel gratitude for it. The aim is to empty your mind of all these negative thoughts and feel good about what is happening around you.

f. Journal writing

Keeping a journal can be a very good way of dealing with your inner critic because it allows you to write down what you think and feels about things. When you write things down, it helps to get rid of the negative thoughts these issues bring up in your mind. Journaling encourages your inner critic to let its thoughts go and releases any negative feelings that may come up. It is also a good way to find out exactly how you are feeling at that moment.

You may also want to include pictures or other things that remind you of what life is like around you. This is a good way to visualize your life and remember the good things while also dealing with negative thoughts that may come up.

g. Stop and think about it!

Sometimes we make things worse by going with our emotions and acting out of fear. Some people don't feel they have the choice to stop this way of thinking and acting because their inner critic is telling them what to do.

But we can stop this process and think things through. You can ask yourself:

- Are these thoughts or feelings real?

- What is the reason for them?

- How likely is it that the things I fear will actually happen?

- Do I need these kinds of reactions and thoughts?

- Is there any way I can change things for the better?

- Is what I am thinking or feeling making sense to me?

- What's the worst that can happen, and is it that bad?

- Why would I give up something good of my own free will just because of a thought or feeling?

- Why would a harmless situation be dangerous just because of bad thoughts or feelings?

When you ask yourself these questions, you can stop yourself from giving in to your inner critic and give yourself some time to think about things. This way, you don't have to act out of fear and impulsiveness because you can think about the situation and then decide for yourself what to do.

Your inner critic is simply a creation of your mind. It is something that isn't real and can't hurt you. It will always try to convince you that it's real and needs to be taken seriously. It will tell you that it won't go away or it will get worse.

But the thing is, you can choose to ignore your inner critic and create a better life for yourself by making different decisions and choices.

4. Other Emotion Regulation Strategies

The following are a few other strategies that may help you deal with your emotions:

a. The Adult Play Technique

The Adult Play Technique is an easy method of dealing with anxiety that involves acting out a scene as though you were in a play. This is an easy and effective way to take control of your emotions.

How to do it:

Step 1: Choose a time when you will be alone for an extended period.

No set amount of time is suggested; just take the amount of time that makes you feel comfortable, and then determine if it is enough or not.

Step 2: Create a character for yourself. You can be anyone you choose.

The personality traits of the character should be very simple. Don't forget to give them a name.

Step 3: Create a situation for your character to be in where they feel anxious or uncomfortable.

This can be as simple as their health being low and them losing energy quickly due to an illness, or as complex as battle wounds from a fight with an evil villain.

Step 4: Let the character do what they will in this deplorable moment.

Try not to think about it too much or let your mind wander into other places during this time. You simply want to observe your character performing each action as if it were your own experience.

This technique can help you gain control of your emotions when you are dealing with anxiety. If you ever need to get control of your emotions and inject some fun into your life so that you don't feel so anxious anymore, this might be the solution.

h. The 30-Minute Challenge

Dismissive avoidants have the hardest time coping with stress because they tend to avoid their anxiety by obsessively thinking negatively.

The 30-Minute Challenge is a technique that helps you deal with your anxiety more productively by confronting your fears head-on, one at a time. It is simple but hard to do, especially with severe anxiety. You only have 30 minutes to overcome your fear; if you don't, you'll have to start over from scratch. This is why it is called a "30-Minute Challenge".

How to do it:

Step 1: Choose a time and place where you will be comfortable and have no distractions.

You can go into your room and close the door or go somewhere else where you will not be interrupted.

Step 2: Think about the issue or situation that scares you.

Focus on the situation that is causing your anxiety.

Step 3: Prepare for the worst by considering the worst-case scenario(s).

Consider what would occur if everything went wrong or how your life would be if everything suddenly stopped working. Think about other scenarios that seem possible and consider how they would affect you or other people involved in the situation(s).

Step 4: Now prepare for the best-case scenario(s) by thinking about what could go right for you.

Think about what you would do if you were in a situation where things went right. Allow yourself to feel the positive emotions that would arise in the best-case scenario.

This technique deals with your fears by confronting them in a certain order. In this way, you can beat your fear by using the power of your imagination. By involving all of your senses (sight, hearing, taste, touch, and smell) in your imaginings, you can deal with your fear and anxiety.

c. Emotion Tagging

Emotion tagging is a very useful exercise that will help you memorize or remember different emotions. This can be especially useful if you're curious about your own emotions and want to be able to express them more clearly. It is also good for people who have trouble identifying their emotions when trying to understand their reactions better.

How to do it:

Step 1: Pick an emotion (or emotions) that you want to learn how to identify.

It can be any emotion you want to learn more about, such as anger, sadness, fear, happiness, disgust, surprise, and even hunger. You could also just pick a single emotion you haven't been able to understand or know better, or perhaps an emotion that has made you feel uncomfortable in the past.

Remember that different emotions may be connected to other emotions. For instance, you might not realize that the person you are angry with is perhaps feeling fear or anxiety as a result of something they are doing incorrectly.

Step 2: Try to bring these different emotions in your mind.

Allow yourself to imagine how this emotion might make your body feel. Try to use all five senses.

Step 3: Try to identify the same emotion in another situation after learning how it feels in your mind.

Once you have identified the emotion in your mind, try to identify it in another situation so that you can label it correctly. To do this effectively, try bringing up all of your senses again since this will help you visualize and understand how someone is feeling. Ask yourself specific questions while identifying the emotion, such as "What does this person look like to you?" or "How do they make you feel?" You can also try describing things to them that you would see, hear, smell, or feel if you were in their position, such as "What do you see in your mind's eye?" or "What does it feel like when you are jealous?"

This technique can be used when trying to identify your own emotions, understanding peers that are describing emotions you do not understand, making other people feel more comfortable talking about their feelings, memorizing emotions for research purposes, or simply learning how to express your emotions properly with others.

d. Self-Hypnosis

This is a very effective tool that can be used to help people focus on a particular task or simply relax. The only limitations of self-hypnosis are your imagination and the amount of time available to you.

How to do it:

Step 1: Get in a comfortable and silent place where nothing will distract you.

You can use a spot that is most familiar to you, such as your bed, couch, or your desk. If you are doing this at a desk, try making yourself as comfortable as possible. You can use a pillow or blanket or even lay your head on your arms to rest more easily. Make sure that nothing will distract you.

Step 2: Pick an image and keep it in mind.

It does not matter what image you pick for yourself; just choose something that it is easy for you to visualize. If you are trying to make yourself relax, then you can pick a relaxing scene like a beach or a garden. If you want to concentrate on something like math for school, picture the numbers and equations in your head as best as possible.

Step 3: Clear your mind of distracting thoughts and concentrate on your image.

Try not to think of anything else while doing this because it will make it harder for you to push those other thoughts out of your head when they start coming in. Try to keep quiet, and try not to let your mind wander off into other things like what you are going to eat for dinner or what you're planning on doing tomorrow. To prevent your mind from wandering, you might also try closing your eyes and imagining yourself in that situation.

Step 4: Relax your body and let go of any tension you might be holding onto.

Try to remain conscious of how your body is feeling right now. If you are concentrating on a beach or a garden, imagine how it would feel to lie down in the sand or grass or how it would smell as if the ocean is nearby. Try to push any uneasy feelings out of your mind and imagine yourself somewhere that your body can relax more readily.

If you are focusing on something that makes you nervous such as math, or something more socially-related such as a party, then try to picture yourself being there and feeling happy and successful. Remember to use all five senses to make the experience as real as possible.

Self-hypnosis can also be beneficial in helping you relax and reduce stress. It can even lower your blood pressure, or even control any pain you might be feeling. The longer the session of self-hypnosis, the more relaxed or concentrated your body will become after doing it.

You can better control your emotions by using a variety of techniques. Learn these techniques and how to use them to help yourself feel better and more comfortable in your own skin. You can also visit a therapist if you want someone to talk about what you are feeling. They can help you devise a plan of action to cope with your feelings in the future. They can also let you know what changes need to be made for things to become more comfortable for you.

Especially as a dismissive avoidant, it can be challenging to express your emotions to others, but these methods and tools can encourage you to do so and make you feel better about what you are going through.

CHAPTER 9

SEEING MYSELF AS OTHERS DO

Dismissive avoidants can sometimes act narcissistically. It's, therefore, important for you to understand how you may come across to others to help facilitate a real change in your behavior.

How Others See Someone with Dismissive Avoidant Attachment

The following are some of the ways people see someone with dismissive avoidant attachment:

1. Reacts badly when others display normal emotions

You may feel in constant control of your emotions, but to others, you may come across as cold and unengaged as you coldly ignore or fluster others.

To further explain...

Emotions cause people to act in certain ways, which is completely normal. For example, when people feel angry, they may raise their voices and act slightly aggressively to express their anger, or when people are upset, they may cry and seek comfort from others. Such emotional expression helps us to understand the other person and their particular needs.

As you know, being a dismissive avoidant makes it difficult for you to process others' emotions correctly. When you see someone else cry or raise their voice, you may not feel comfortable approaching them. This is because you do not understand the normal range of human emotion and instead feel threatened that the other person may be behaving aggressively or controllingly. Therefore, if you see someone upset, you may appear distant. You may speak very matter-of-factly toward them and tell them to calm down. You may even raise your voice at them if they do not comply with your request. This will lead to more distress for the other person because they don't understand why you behave this way.

It's difficult for others to understand that sometimes when you are dismissive avoidant, there is a reason for your behavior, and most of the time, it's because of your issues rather than anything else. However, most people don't know about the dismissive-avoidant attachment style and will not understand when you behave like this.

2. May come across as self-centered

It's not uncommon for you to be preoccupied with your problems and needs at the expense of others. Dismissive avoidants may appear self-centered to others because they only focus on themselves and their problems.

To further explain...

The dismissive-avoidant approach to life is very self-centered and insular. You may find it difficult to focus on the other person when speaking to them. Instead, you may focus on your thoughts and concerns, which can come across as self-centered and narcissistic.

When conversing with someone else, it's usually because they have asked a question or made a statement which has caused you to think about how it applies to your life. You may only focus on yourself, so you will appear selfish.

3. Antisocial

The dismissive-avoidant attachment style is characterized by the inability to form relationships and socialize properly so you may come across as antisocial. This is because you don't understand what it takes to relate to other people on an emotional level and so you miss out on many of life's joys.

To further explain...

You may appear very antisocial to others, but this can be unintentional and caused by your issues. Often people are concerned about you and would like to spend more time with you, but you don't want them there for fear that they might interfere in your life. You may not see them as a support network because you fear they will always want to be involved in your life and threaten your independence.

It's important to understand that when people are concerned about you and attempt to spend time with you, it is usually a sign that they respect and care for you.

4. Pessimist

Sometimes people see you as a pessimist. They may think you are very negative and have low expectations because you expect failure and misery in whatever you do.

To further explain...

You may come across as a pessimist when struggling with your interpersonal relationships. You probably don't want to talk about how there is no hope for the future, and prolonged suffering awaits, but you nonetheless believe it's better to prepare yourself for this reality. You are realistic in that you don't let yourself get your hopes up, and you won't be disappointed when things turn out a certain way. You know others can be unpredictable, so accepting whatever happens without preconceived expectations is better. It might appear to others that you are too negative, but they don't understand how people can be unpredictable, or that it can often let you down in the worst possible way. Life can be difficult and painful, as we all know, but you feel that if you know this ahead of time, you will be prepared for what is to come and are therefore not disappointed when it happens.

5. Critical

People may see you as critical and judgmental. They may feel you are harsh and may not want to be around you anymore because something about your character rubs them up the wrong way.

To further explain...

You might seem critical and judgmental because you always see other people's faults. You notice their mistakes and believe they should have done things differently, but this is not necessarily the case. When you see other people do or say something that they shouldn't have done or should not have said, this doesn't mean that they are evil. Everyone makes mistakes, and you need to allow for this. Being critical when it's unnecessary will cause you more problems than it will solve.

When you are critical, you tend to feel negative and waste time focusing on others and their mistakes. You are looking for them to change and do things a certain way, but usually, this isn't possible. You may not want to be critical, but it is often the only way you believe things can improve for everyone involved. If others were to get too close to your life, they would be able to learn what goes on behind closed doors and would then be able to determine why you act so critically.

When others make mistakes, you must remain calm and let them manage their own issues. You don't want to be seen as a bad person who is trying to bring other people down.

6. Aggressive

Others may see you as either aggressive or angry, and they often don't want to be around you because they feel threatened.

To further explain...

You may be seen as aggressive, and people may be afraid of you. You have the potential to be a very destructive force in someone else's life if you let your anger loose or if it gets out of control. Because people don't want to risk becoming the target of your aggression, they will avoid you at all costs.

You might feel physically aggressive because of your anger towards someone as a result of something they have done to you. You might feel that you are justified in being angry towards them and that it's okay to be aggressive, but this is not true. When you get angry and lash out at other people, it's like having a monkey on your back that won't let go until the person who has made you angry sees the error of their ways. But when people feel intimidated by you, they have no choice but to put their safety above anything else and avoid you in order to protect themselves from further damage.

You might also be seen as aggressive if you are constantly in a bad mood and are always finding reasons to be angry and cynical because that's all you know. You may never have experienced good feelings, so your entire life is filled with negativity and anger. It's often the case that people feel they have no choice but to avoid you because they don't want to get involved with your negative approach towards life, or they are worried that they will become victims of your aggression. They don't want to risk being hurt by your words if they say something that triggers you. They know it's all too easy for you to take your anger out on them and then never look back.

7. Unreliable

People may see you as unreliable because they cannot trust you to do what you say or promise. They may feel confused and think there is more behind the scenes than meets the eye, but nobody knows exactly what's happening with you.

To further explain...

If you have a track record of going back on your word, people will become suspicious and wonder what is going on with you. They won't know if they can trust you to do what you say or if they should believe everything you're telling them. It will become normal for them to question whether or not you are genuine and trustworthy.

Being a dismissive avoidant means not paying attention to other people's feelings, which means that you may not notice, or perhaps you don't care about, the fact that people are losing trust in you. You won't understand why they are doing this because your ego will blind you. You may feel that you are right and they are wrong, or you may feel that it is for the best for everyone for you to go your separate ways, especially if you fear becoming too vulnerable around them. Others will often begin to see this behavior as manipulative and domineering, or they may even become scared because you are controlling them. They will likely lose a great deal of their trust in you.

People may also see you as unreliable if it becomes apparent that your behavior might create problems for others. People will no longer want to engage with you because there is no point in doing so when the consequences can be so negative.

8. Lazy

People may think you are lazy and unwilling to aid in their personal development because you don't want to invest energy into doing things for them. You may not care enough about helping people out, especially if they are weak or have trouble achieving what they want.

To further explain...

You may be perceived as lazy if you believe that others are capable of doing things on their own when they are not; in such a case, it may be your responsibility to assist them. They may feel like you are lazy because you aren't willing to help them get what they want.

If people see that you never put much effort into getting other people out of a rut, they will wonder if they can trust you to help them with anything in the future. They will wonder if you have written them off because they have become incapable of doing anything. They will lose trust in you and come to believe there is nothing left to invest in their relationship with you.

9. Immoral

People may see you as immoral because they feel your behavior is going against the grain or that it doesn't match up to what is considered normal.

To further explain...

You may be seen as immoral if you are doing things that are widely considered against the grain. People label these actions as immoral because they deviate from social norms and leave a bad taste in people's mouths. It may cause them to avoid you because they did not antici-pate seeing such behavior from you.

The word "immoral" is a very strong word that can be pretty scary if other people start to accuse you of being so. When people see you being immoral, they will start to feel like they can't trust you because they believe there is something wrong with the way that you think or act. They may find your behavior to be in poor taste and be perplexed as to why this is happening. They might blame themselves for doing something to encourage this kind of behavior from you, or they may start to lose respect for you and lose faith in your friendship.

10. Immature

When people think you are immature, they may lose faith in what you have to say or believe. You may have a reputation for being immature because you do things that are not appropriate, and this goes against what most people would do.

To further explain...

You may be seen as immature if you don't act like a "normal" adult, especially when making life decisions. They will then start to doubt whether they can trust you. They may even be afraid of you acting immature one day and endangering their lives in some way.

When people see you acting immature, they will question why you feel the need to act in such a way. It is important to know that these judgments can be made about you, as a result of your attachment style. Despite this, you can still have a good relationship with others if you know how to manage it properly.

PART 4

LOVING A DISMISSIVE-AVOIDANT PARTNER

CHAPTER 10

PRACTICAL TIPS FOR HELPING A LOVED ONE WITH DISMISSIVE-AVOIDANT TRAITS

L oving a dismissive-avoidant partner is difficult but possible. There are a number of strategies to build your relationship with someone who possesses these traits.

It won't be easy—and the process may not be immediate or short-term—but it is possible. If you make an effort, both of you will benefit. You'll have a deeper, more satisfying relationship than if you don't.

The following are some practical tips you can use to help the dismissive-avoidant person in your life:

1. Be a good communicator

Avoid changing the subject when they start talking about their feelings. Listen intently and ask appropriate questions to show that you're interested in what they're saying.

Being a good communicator goes beyond just listening well. It means allowing the other person to feel comfortable enough with you to be open and honest about their emotions, fears, and desires.

How to do this:

The following are some techniques you can practice to help a loved one with dismissive avoidant traits feel comfortable enough to communicate:

a. Share your feelings & express your needs

Try expressing your own needs and feelings during regular conversations. This shows the other person that you're not going to ignore their feelings but allows them to feel that their emotions are also valid and deserve to be heard.

The following are some examples of helpful ways to express your own emotions:

- "I feel sad when I see you leaving home after a difficult fight or argument."

- "I feel embarrassed when you tell others that I don't do my chores around the house."

- "Sometimes I feel angry or hurt when you do that, but I don't like to tell you."

- "I often feel anxious when we're in a crowded place like at a shopping mall or on the subway."

- "I feel happy when you agree to be my partner at a dinner party."

- "Occasionally, I wish we could spend more time together."

Sharing your feelings with the person you love will help them see that they have just as much right as you to share their feelings as you do.

b. Express understanding and empathy

If you're talking to someone with dismissive-avoidant traits, you must show that you understand their feelings.

Here are some examples of appropriate ways to show this understanding:

- "Hearing you say that is difficult. I understand how you feel."

- "I realize how challenging it is for you to say that. I'm sorry your recent struggles have been so difficult."

- "It must be stressful when we argue sometimes. We both have difficulty communicating about our expectations for this relationship."

- "You seem sad whenever we're in a crowded place like at a shopping mall or on the subway. You probably don't want to

be here where it's always so busy, but I know it's not easy for
you to say no to going with me when I ask you to accompany
me to places like these."

- "It's painful to see you so sad. I'm sorry that you're having a
hard time right now."

- "I understand your fears about moving away from your family, but I hope we can work it out."

Asking questions is also a good way to express your understanding and
empathy:

- "You seem upset now, and I'd like to know what makes you
feel that way."

- "I'd like to ask what you're afraid of right now."

- "I've noticed that you seem depressed. Do you have any needs
that I can assist you with?"

- "It must be painful when we argue sometimes, and I'd like to
ask why that is so hard for you."

Understanding and expressing empathy show that you're trying to
"walk in the other person's shoes," so to speak. This can help them
feel comfortable opening up to you and sharing their feelings.

c. Be an active listener

Active listening is sometimes called "reflective listening," which means
you should repeat the important points that the other person said

back to them. This is a useful technique to demonstrate that you are paying attention to what they are saying and that you recognize their emotions.

How can you do this?

Step 1: Make eye contact with your conversation partner.

Making eye contact shows them that you're paying attention to what they're saying and reinforces the idea that their feelings are important to you.

Step 2: Try repeating what they said back to them in your own words

This shows them that you're listening to them and understand their feelings.

Don't interrupt or change the subject while they talk; repeat what they've said after they've finished speaking.

Step 3: Ask for clarification when necessary

Sometimes it may not be easy to understand what the other person is saying, so try asking for more examples or details. This demonstrates your interest in what they have to say and shows that you're interested in learning more about what's going on for them. Make an effort to look at their eyes when responding so they know you are listening to what they say. However, ensure not to interrupt or ask too many questions, as this can make the other person feel rushed and uncomfortable.

Your questions may include:

- "Could you tell me more about the 'things' you're talking about?"

- "How did you come to that conclusion?"

- "What happened exactly?"

- "Why do you say that?"

- "How would you define that?"

- "Can you say exactly what it was that upset you?"

Of course, this is a fairly simple technique; it just takes practice to stay focused and not interrupt or ask too many questions.

Step 4: Summarize what they've said

After they've finished talking, check that you understood by summarizing what they've just said in your own words. This shows that you understand their feelings and highlights important points from the conversation.

Active listening is a good way of showing that you're interested in what they have to say and want to understand their feelings as much as they do. It encourages them to share their feelings and helps build trust and reduce conflict.

In a relationship, communication is crucial since it helps the other person comprehend our thoughts and feelings. Communicating with an avoidant-dismissive partner is difficult because they tend to be emotionally unavailable. However, you can still try your best to understand how they feel and why they are acting the way they are.

2. Try to avoid issuing ultimatums

An ultimatum can cause tensions to flare up and push the person you love away. Even if ultimatums often work in the short term, they aren't fair or helpful to the other person.

Instead, try to work out fair and forgiving solutions after a misunderstanding or disagreement as soon as possible.

The following are some examples of unfair and unhelpful ultimatums that you can avoid.

a. The "silent treatment."

If you're furious with the person you love, the silent treatment could seem like a good idea, but it usually just makes matters worse.

How can you avoid this?

1. Think about how the person you love is feeling and why.

Everyone reacts to situations differently, so it's important to understand why they might be upset instead of criticizing them for getting angry. This can help lessen their frustration and anger.

2. Stay calm

Try to avoid getting angry with them, and don't blame or criticize them for feeling the way they do. If you can keep your cool, it will benefit both of you.

3. Talk to them directly, if possible; if not, write a letter or e-mail instead

If possible, talk to the person you love directly when upset; if they're having trouble calming down, try writing a letter or e-mail expressing how you feel instead of having a face-to-face confrontation. Sometimes it helps to put your feelings into words, as this can give you a fresh perspective.

It can be hard to communicate directly with someone when one or both of you are angry, so it's important to remember that even if you speak to them, they might find it difficult to calm down. They might need some time to feel secure enough to open up to you, which will also give you some time to collect yourself.

The silent treatment is not a good way to deal with conflict. Even if it helps you calm down and think about what you're going to do, it can cause long-term problems in the relationship.

Ultimatums in relationships create unnecessary tension and conflict, build resentment and ill-will, destroying the intimacy and trust between the two parties. Ultimatums are generally unsuitable in a relationship because they are not fair and don't allow both partners to be treated as equals. Some people think that ultimatums show how much they care about their partner, but this is not always true.

b. The "do this or else."

This is a common tactic for behavior modification, and it often doesn't work because the consequences aren't realistic. If a problem crops up again in the future, it's likely to cause more issues between you. Some studies show that people avoid communication in these situations, so things get worse instead of better.

How can you avoid this?

1. Don't give orders

Instead, listen to why the problem occurred and try to understand their feelings. Try not to blame them for what happened because this may make it more difficult for them to apologize and reassure you.

2. Be forgiving, and suggest a compromise instead of an ultimatum or punishment

If the person you love has made a mistake, then try to think of ways that they can resolve the problem that will make things better in the future instead of punishing them for making a mistake. For example, if they forget an important event (e.g., birthday or anniversary), see if there's anything they can do to make up for it and prevent it from happening again.

3. Don't play mind games

This can be very hurtful since the person you love may feel confused and will not know how to respond properly. It also makes them less likely to trust you and they may feel like you're trying to control them rather than make things better between you. This may cause the person to feel trapped in a relationship and unwilling to communicate properly. This can make them question if they want any relationship with you or if you mean as much to them as they do to you.

c. The "one-up, one-down" strategy

This involves doing small favors, often repeatedly, to keep the other person indebted to you. This makes it easier for you to ask for bigger favors later, even if they aren't related to the initial problem.

The fact that you ultimately get what you want may make this seem like a good idea, but it's not a fair way to communicate, and it can put too much stress on your relationship.

How can you avoid this?

1. Be fair and honest.

Don't give or ask for favors that aren't important, and don't expect the other person to feel indebted to you.

2. Don't string together favors or make a big deal out of small issues.

Before requesting assistance once more, ask yourself if you really need it; consider whether you can complete the task yourself rather than asking someone for a favor.

3. Don't force the other person to choose between you and someone else.

If they feel like they have to choose between you and another person, they might resent you because they have no freedom of choice. This can make it more difficult for them to deal with the issue because it makes them feel trapped in the relationship.

The "one-up, one-down" strategy can hurt your relationship if you don't keep the other person's needs in mind. They might feel compelled to try to mend things between you two because they believe they have no other option, which could make them even more resentful of you than they already are. This can make them question whether having a relationship with you is worth it.

d. The "take it or leave it" strategy

This is often the result of a person feeling taken for granted or ignored in the relationship, so they withdraw from interaction to see what the other person will do.

Another common reason for using this strategy is when a person feels they have no control of the situation and no voice in what goes on between them. This strategy can be frustrating because it can cause a lot of tension and conflict between the people involved.

How can you avoid this?

1. Communicate your feelings and needs

Just because you're not getting what you want doesn't mean that the other person doesn't care about you or respect you. If the issue is annoying or difficult, don't just accept it passively; communicate to the other person what is bothering them. Be sincere and prepared to make concessions to improve things between the two of you.

2. Listen to your partner when they express their needs and emotions.

It is not easy to hear that you're not treating someone the way they would like to be treated. However, if the relationship is important to both of you, try to listen to what they have said. Be willing and open to changing yourself to make things better between the two of you.

3. Don't blame or resent your partner if they are unhappy with something in the relationship

Suppose they have come forth with a problem or issue between you. In that case, it is usually due to their concern for how things are going in your relationship, so remember to keep the other person's feelings in mind when you communicate.

The "take it or leave it" strategy can be very hurtful and frustrating for you and your partner; it can cause some people to stop communicating with their partner because they don't want to deal with the constant arguing and frustration that results from this kind of relationship.

CONCLUSION

Our attachment styles result from our early experiences with parents, caregivers, and other significant relationships. In addition to the psychological effects caused by these early relationships, some of us may also develop certain character traits, such as dismissive-avoidant attachment, which are more difficult to overcome.

It is important to understand the causes and consequences of dismissive-avoidant attachment and to know yourself in order to overcome this type of behavior. The first step in overcoming these behaviors is recognizing them and understanding what they are doing to your life. Once you understand why you have these tendencies and behaviors, you can find ways to overcome them by learning new skills and behaviors and developing new habits.

Dismissive-avoidant attachment can be difficult to overcome. This combination is not uncommon in children raised in a family with a history of abuse, neglect, or chaotic attachment relationships. The characteristics that contribute to dismissive-avoidant attachment include difficulty being assertive, over-dependent and clingy behavior, difficulty communicating and expressing emotions, being overly self-conscious, low self-esteem, and adopting certain behaviors to ensure no one will harm you again. These tendencies are formed early on in life and carry over into adulthood. The combination makes it very difficult for the individual to successfully create successful and rewarding relationships.

However, just as there is a wide range of behaviors and feelings associated with dismissive-avoidant attachment, many ways exist to overcome it. The most common changes involve making sense of your relationships, developing communication and self-regulation skills, expressing your feelings and emotions, challenging negative thoughts and behaviors that may be holding you back, and creating a solid relationship with yourself.

A successful relationship with another person is simpler once you alter your self-perception and consider the way others perceive you. This step allows you to have a better idea of what your partner's needs are and how you can meet those needs. In addition, the more secure and confident you feel in relationships, the less likely you will be attracted to a person with the same insecure attachment pattern.

The bottom line is if you want a successful relationship, it helps to understand what makes relationships successful and what challenges you may face. If you understand yourself and your attachment style better, you can improve your interactions with others and, over time, become more comfortable creating successful relationships.